Canada's National Child Benefit

Canada's National Child Benefit

Phoenix or Fizzle?

edited by
Douglas Durst

Fernwood Publishing

In memory, Emily Mary Durst, 1918–1998.

Editing: Todd Scarth
Cover photo: Rob Barrow; concept: "Cuts are Hurting Our Kids" by Cathy Collins, Greg Selinger and students of Inner City Social Work program, 1993–94, Winnipeg Education Centre.
Design and production: Beverley Rach
Printed and bound in Canada by: Hignell Printing Limited

A publication of:
Fernwood Publishing
Box 9409, Station A
Halifax, Nova Scotia
B3K 5S3

This book has been supported by the Division of Employability and Social Partnerships, Human Resources Development Canada and the Social Policy Research Unit, Faculty of Social Work, University of Regina. (The views expressed in this book do not necessarily represent those of the Employability and Social Partnership Division.)

Fernwood Publishing Company Limited gratefully acknowledges the financial support of the Ministry of Canadian Heritage and the Canada Council for the Arts for our publishing program.

Canadian Cataloguing in Publication Data

Main entry under title:

Canada's national child benefit

    Includes bibliographical references.
    ISBN 1-55266-009-5

1. Family allowance -- Canada.   2. Federal aid to child welfare -- Canada.
3. Income maintenance programs -- Canada.   4. Poor children -- Canada.
I. Durst, Douglas.

HV745.A6C27 1999   362.82820971   C99-950010-4

Contents

Acknowledgements

There are many people to thank but first of all, it is important to recognize the contributors to this volume for their participation and diligence in re-drafting conference papers into book chapters. Without their careful intellectual work followed by a commitment to share their ideas, there would be no book.

I am grateful to the Employability and Social Partnerships Division of Human Resources Development Canada for its support of the Eighth Conference on Canadian Social Welfare Policy, held in Regina from June 25–28, 1997. In particular, I wish to acknowledge the support from Evariste Theriault and Sandra Chatterton and look forward to future endeavours in applied research in Canadian social policy.

Numerous key individuals were involved in the planning and delivery of this highly successful conference. Jan Joel, Research Co-ordinator of the Social Policy Research Unit, Faculty of Social Work, University of Regina, provided exceptional leadership and commitment to the success of the conference. Much credit must be given to her and I wish her well in her new work with the Saskatchewan, Status of Women. Special thanks to Dave Broad, Faculty of Social Work in Regina, for his patient and gentle leadership. In addition, Linda Bradley provided solid administrative support for the conference and this publication.

Members of the Conference Steering Committee included Dave Broad, University of Regina, Paul Leduc Browne, Canadian Centre for Policy Alternatives, Sandra Chatterton, Employability and Social Partnerships, Michael Goldberg, Social Planning Council of B.C., Jan Joel, formerly of the University of Regina, Sharon McKay, University of Regina, Terry Mountjoy, Social Development Association of Social Workers, Geoff Pawson, Saskatchewan Association of Social Workers, Jane Pulkingham, Simon Fraser University, Gordon Ternowetsky, University of Northern British Columbia, Neil Yeates, Saskatchewan Social Services, and me.

Thank you too for Corinne Herne's computer expertise in preparing the chapters for the final editorial review. Wayne Antony of Fernwood Publishing provided guidance and insight in the details of publication and made sure we all met our deadlines. Thanks also to all those whose work has transformed the manuscript into a book: to Todd Scarth for his skillful copy editing; to Beverley Rach for designing and setting the pages and for designing the cover; to Debbie Mathers for typing the final changes to the manuscript; and to Brenda Conroy for proofreading.

Douglas Durst

About the Contributors

Douglas Durst is a professor of social work in the Faculty of Social Work at the University of Regina. He has many years experience in the practice of social work and social research in partnership with Aboriginal and First Nations people. He has published collaboratively numerous articles and chapters dealing with issues of self-government of social services and the empowering process of First Nations. He is currently researching the triple jeopardy of urban First Nations persons with disabilities.

Rick August is currently Senior Policy Advisor for Income Security Programs with Saskatchewan Social Services in Regina. He is a member of the National Child Benefit Working Group, the committee of government officials from various federal, provincial and territorial agencies which negotiated and designed the initiative, and chaired several NCB implementation sub-committees. He has been employed by the Government of Saskatchewan in various research and policy capacities since 1974.

Ken Battle is President of the Caledon Institute of Social Policy, an independent social policy think tank based in Ottawa. Educated at Queen's and Oxford, he is one of Canada's leading social policy thinkers. He served on the Ministerial Task Force on Social Security Reform in 1994 and as an advisor on child benefits reform to the Minister of Human Resources Development in 1996 and 1997. Battle has published widely on social policy issues, including income security, taxation, medicare, social services and poverty. He wrote the influential "Social Policy by Stealth" and "Limits to Social Policy" to name only two of his many contributions to social policy debate.

Michael Birmingham, has a doctorate in Social Work from the University of Toronto and is presently the executive director of Carlington Community and Health Services, a community health centre in Ottawa. His recent research interests have focused on the nature of work and unpaid labour.

Pete Hudson is an associate professor at the Faculty of Social Work, University of Manitoba. He has taught and conducted research in social work and policy in regard to Aboriginal people, child welfare, community development and social administration. He has co-ordinated the preparation of the Manitoba Alternative Budget for the past two years on behalf of Cho!ces: A Coalition for Social Justice. Recent publications included "Welfare Pluralism in the U.K.: Views from the Voluntary Sector" in *Canadian Review of Social Policy*, Spring 1998. "The voluntary sector, the state and citizenship in the U.K." will appear in *Social Service Review*, December 1998.

Jane Pulkingham is an associate professor of sociology at Simon Fraser University. Her teaching and research interests are in the area of feminist political economy of the welfare state, gender and social policy, employment and income security policy and family law (the economics of divorce). With Gordon Ternowetsky, she edited *Remaking of Canadian Social Policy: Social Security in the Late 1990s* and *Child and Family Policies: Struggles, Strategies and Options* both with Fernwood Publishing.

Karen Swift is an associate professor at the School of Social Work, York University. She was the author of *Manufacturing of Bad Mothers: A Critical Perspective on Child Neglect*, as well as other chapters and articles concerned with issues of child welfare. Her work over many years has also focused on social policy analysis especially in relation to poverty and contemporary women's issues.

Gordon Ternowetsky is a professor of social work at the University of Northern British Columbia. His research and teaching interests are in the area of unemployment, poverty, and social policy and social work. He is a founding editor of *Australian Canadian Studies* and is co-ordinator of the Child Welfare Research Centre at UNBC. With Graham Riches, he edited *Unemployment and Welfare: Social Policy and the Work of Social Work* (Garamond Press). With Jane Pulkingham, he edited *Remaking of Canadian Social Policy: Social Security in the Late 1990s* and *Child and Family Policies: Struggles, Strategies and Options* both with Fernwood Publishing.

Preface

In June 1997, the faculty of the University of Regina hosted the Eighth Conference on Canadian Social Welfare Policy. During the conference a number of interesting and challenging papers were presented that examined the issues regarding child poverty and the federal promise of a national program to move children out of the welfare rolls. The $850 million promised by the federal government represented a significant return to federal involvement in social programs. After a litany of cuts, slashes and "clawbacks," it had been over thirty years since Canadians had seen a new federal social program.

This book attempts to outline the key concepts of this new program and set the stage for discussion of its potential impact. Is this new program a "phoenix," the rise of the federal government from the ashes of the former devastated programs, or is it a "fizzle," a sputtering noise with little long-term effect? The following chapters do not agree. This book does not present a unified argument either supporting or critiquing the program but raises a series of important issues and concerns regarding the program's effectiveness in addressing child poverty.

The opening chapter attempts to set the stage for discussion. The first section outlines some of the central issues of the program and presents some background information, such as the meaning of the terms "child" and "poverty lines." Tables and graphs demonstrate the patterns of poverty historically, geographically and by family type. In recent years, poverty among children has been increasing in both numbers and depth.

Ken Battle, head of the Caledon Institute of Social Policy, has been a longstanding advocate for an integrated child benefit strategy for addressing child poverty and breaking down the welfare wall. His chapter clearly presents the details of the National Child Benefit System and argues for its support as a realistic alternative to past practices which trapped many individuals in stigmatizing welfare.

Rick August, a senior policy analyst with the Saskatchewan government, looks at his province's innovations to the program and its effectiveness at encouraging and supporting working families. He argues that the combined National Child Benefit System puts most families ahead.

Karen Swift of York University and Michael Birmingham, Carlington Community and Health Services, provide a comprehensive gender analysis examining the impact of poverty on women and children and the implications of the National Child Benefit System. Their chapter includes an important theoretical discussion on the ideologies of work and its impacts on single mothers. They report the qualitative findings of three groups of single women on social assistance thereby providing the reader with the human side of poverty. The discussion provides a critical assessment of the program and its affect on women.

Jane Pulkingham, Simon Fraser University, and Gordon Ternowetsky, University of Northern British Columbia, have co-edited two important books on the social policy debate from previous social policy conferences. They offer a more critical discussion of the program and its impact on those Canadians who have difficulty finding employment that provides sufficient remuneration. They argue that the program does not offer any new monies from the federal government and is really a disguised incentive program pushing people into a type of workfare.

Clearly these contributors do not agree and offer a challenging and stimulating debate. In the concluding chapter, Pete Hudson of the University of Manitoba pulls the arguments together, highlighting the contributors' areas of agreement and points of departure. He also sets the context within the larger picture of international capital. The question remains: Is this new federal social program a phoenix rising from the ashes of past social welfare programs or just a federal fizzle? Please join the debate!

Douglas Durst

1

Phoenix or Fizzle?
Background to Canada's New National Child Benefit

Douglas Durst

> **phoenix**: (myth) bird, the only one of its kind, that after living five or six centuries in the Arabian desert burnt itself on a funeral pile and rose from the ashes with renewed youth to live through another cycle; paragon.
> **fizzle**: hiss or splutter feebly; come to lame conclusion.
> —*The Concise Oxford Dictionary*

In the past decade, Canadians have proudly celebrated their high grades from the United Nations' ratings of human development, but quietly ignored the fact that Canada ranks among the worst of all major Western countries in rates of child poverty. In 1996, 1.4 million children lived in poverty (one out of five), which was a 46 percent increase from 1989. This introductory chapter presents key data on the dimensions of child and family poverty in Canada, showing the increasing rates of poverty in light of government's token efforts to eliminate it. Rates of poverty vary between the provinces and even within some cities where ghettos have begun to emerge.

Although, on the whole, Canadian children enjoy good health, there are some disturbing trends, such as increased smoking among teenage girls and decreased physical activity among all groups. Poverty is directly related to health status, just as it influences such things as access to quality food, prenatal care and risks of death, injury and disability from trauma and environment. Children from poor families are less likely to survive their first year of life, and the infant mortality rate is four times the national average among Aboriginal families. In addition, children living in poverty fare poorly in all measures of educational and social development. The situation is not new. As a 1975 study by the National Council of Welfare succinctly stated,

> To be born poor is to face a greater likelihood of ill health—in

infancy, in childhood and throughout your adult life. To be born poor is to face a lesser likelihood that you will finish high school; lesser still that you will attend university. To be born poor is to face a greater likelihood that you will be judged a delinquent in adolescence and, if so, a greater likelihood that you will be sent to a "correctional institution." To be born poor is to have the deck stacked against you at birth, to find life an uphill struggle ever after. To be born poor is unfair to kids. (NCW 1975:1)

Phoenix or Fizzle? The New Child Benefit System

Following the Second World War, Canadians enjoyed the development of a substantial social infrastructure, including unemployment insurance, health insurance, a national pension plan and a social assistance program based on the Canada Assistance Plan. These social welfare programs were rooted in a belief in social justice and fairness and assumptions based on Keynesian economics, which argued that government interventions stimulated and encouraged growth and prosperity. Over the years, a comprehensive "social safety net" was created to support citizens who were disadvantaged through unemployment, under-employment, disability, education, poverty and so on.

In regard to poverty, the Canada Assistance Plan (CAP) of 1966 ensured every Canadian had a right to the basic needs of life such as food, clothing and shelter. The program created national standards, and although there were modest provincial differences in delivery, the program was essentially the same in all regions of the country. It was a cost-shared program between the provinces and the federal government, ensuring a commitment from both parties. However, it was a welfare program and suffered the limitation of insufficient assistance to truly facilitate self-sufficiency and independence. It was also based on the indignity of a means-test which processed individuals based on pre-determined need.

Since the 1980s, this safety net has suffered a gradual and subtle attack through a series of clawbacks and de-indexing. Clawbacks refer to situations in which the federal or provincial governments recover benefits through taxation based upon the income levels of the individual. De-indexing refers to the failure to increase benefits to account for inflation. If benefits are held at a given level and the annual inflation rate is, for example, 5 percent, then there is a corresponding actual decrease in benefits. Over time, the benefit becomes less significant. Battle (1990) described this attack on the social welfare system as "social policy by stealth."

The past two decades have seen the debate shift from a Keynesian argument based on social fairness to a Reagan/Thatcher position which argues that less government is better government and has instigated a fiscal-restraint hysteria. Budget- and deficit-cutting have become an obsession for both federal and provincial governments.

In the federal budget of 1995, Finance Minister Paul Martin announced the demise of the Canada Assistance Plan and the introduction of the Canada Health and Social Transfer Act (CHST). It effectively eliminated 40 percent of the federal–provincial transfer payments for health care, social assistance and post-secondary education (Clarke 1998:64). More than reducing the amount of monies in the transfer payments, the new Act terminated the long-standing cost-sharing structures and the commitment that the monies would be used to assist those in poverty: "Federal transfer payments would be made in the form of a much smaller block grant, allowing the provinces to decide what amounts are allocated to health, education and social assistance" (Clarke 1998:67). The provincial governments came under public pressure to apply the reduced transfer payments to health and education. With no national standards to protect their interests and, in a neo-liberal political climate, marginalized persons, such as those with disabilities, the working poor and those depending upon social assistance, saw decreased benefits. In addition to decreasing benefits, provincial governments have been testing workfare approaches, forcing assistance recipients into low-paying jobs subsidized by public money.

By the late 1990s, the federal government found itself with an improving fiscal situation resulting from the various program cuts and increasing tax revenues. With over 1.4 million children in poverty, an earlier pledge to end child poverty had become an albatross for the federal government. As a result, Finance Minister Paul Martin announced $850 million for a new child program, effective July 1, 1998, and a further $850 million as an election promise (a total of $1.7 billion by the year 2000). These monies would be added to the existing $5.1 billion in the child tax credit program. The principle idea of the new program was to move 1.2 million children out of the welfare system, which had become stigmatized as the means-tested "dole." It was estimated that 2.5 million children in low-income families, both working and on social assistance, would receive some benefits. The program would increase federal benefits for over 1.4 million families, whose incomes were below the $25,921 threshold.

The program was meant to increase the financial resources of children and remove the barrier many poor families encounter attempting to enter the employment market. By accepting low-paying jobs, families on social assistance could lose supplementary benefits, such as non-insured health benefits like medications and dental services. The potential loss of these benefits had created a barrier for families on social assistance, and the new program was thought to tear down Canada's "welfare wall" (*Globe and Mail* June 19, 1998, A6). The "welfare wall" is a term created by the Caledon Institute of Social Policy in 1993 to describe the barriers welfare recipients experience leaving the security of regular social assistance and entering the employment market. The loss of both cash and in-kind benefits was not compensated by employment, which can include increased costs such as day care and a long list of pay deductions. The intent was for poor children to gradually move out of the means-test programs into a benefit system of support. The program was not designed to separate from provincial programs, but instead to dove-tail into these programs. The federal Child Tax Benefit was changed into the new Canada Child Tax Benefit, which saves the provinces about $510 million in social assistance costs. These savings were to be returned to support low-income families with children through special programs and services. The combination of the federal Canada Child Tax Benefit (CCTB) and provincial programs became the new National Child Benefit System (NCBS).

Although the reinvestment plan varies slightly among the provinces, the basic concept is shared and lies in its income support for working families. While the benefits for families on welfare remain constant, benefits for working families are supplemented by sums from $2,000 to $5,000, depending on income and family size, thereby breaking the welfare wall. In Ontario, families with net incomes under $25,921 receive a child benefit of $605 a year for each child under eighteen. However, those families on social assistance have their cheques cut by an amount equal to the child benefit; hence, social assistance recipients will see no increase, giving incentive to enter the employment market. No one is supposed to be any worse off than before the plan; only those working will see any gains in family resources. Unfortunately, the plan creates two types of poor families: those who are gainfully employed and those who are not.

This federal initiative is significant in that it is the first new national social program in thirty years. For three decades the federal government resorted to tampering with and reducing those programs created in the postwar period. The new money for poor children has been welcomed by provincial governments, anti-poverty groups and the general public. Is the program a phoenix, the mighty federal government rising from the ashes of the great social welfare era of the postwar period? Or is it a fizzle, no more than a splutter with little real impact on the poverty of Canadian children; too little too late?

Anti-poverty groups herald any government efforts to reduce poverty and assist those economically marginalized. However, critics of the program point to five distinct deficiencies. First, the discrimination of dividing the poor into working and non-working is discouraging for many individuals who lack the skills or abilities to find a job or who live in economically depressed regions.

Second, the program will assist 50 percent of two-parent, low-income families and only 12 percent of single-parent low-income families. Obviously, with one parent providing child care, two-parent families have an easier time entering the workforce and thereby receiving benefits. Since most single-parent families are headed by women, there is systemic bias against single mothers.

Third, First Nations leaders and Aboriginal activists have stated their opposition to the new program and called for exemption for First Nations people. At the annual convention of the Assembly of First Nations, on June 24, 1998, First Nations leaders pointed out that the program is targeted for the working poor and many Native people are trapped in communities where there are few employment opportunities. They fear that there will be less money for families on welfare (*Regina Leader Post* June 25, 1998, A2). Grand Chief of the Assembly Phil Fontaine stated, "We are determined to reduce the dependency on welfare, but we don't want to be victimized by this" (*Regina Leader Post* June 25, 1998, A2). As with single mothers, the program has a systemic bias against many First Nations and Aboriginal families.

Fourth, the program is expected to move 3,000 Ontario families over the income line for social assistance eligibility. Once off the social assistance program, these 3,000 families will lose drug, dental and vision benefits. In response to their situation, Ontario Minister Janet Ecker promised that her ministry will help those "negatively impacted" (*Toronto Star* June 19, 1998, A6), in the belief that no family should be worse off under the new program.

Finally, people on social assistance often work; they move in and out of income-producing activities such as home businesses, seasonal employment, temporary positions and part-time jobs. Most recipients of social assistance have diversified incomes of which social assistance is only one part. The impact of the new NCBS on many of these people is therefore limited.

There is another major issue that may reduce this potential phoenix to a fizzle. The *Constitution Act* (1982) clearly designates social programs as a provincial jurisdiction. Even before the July 1, 1998, implementation date, the provincial premiers were posturing to carefully guard their political domains.

The June 18, 1998, edition of the *Ottawa Citizen* printed an article with the following headline: "Premiers move to restrict new federal social programs" (A2). It was evident that the premiers' concerns were stimulated by the NCBS. Apparently, the provincial finance ministers had met to develop a plan "to severely restrict the federal government's ability to create new national social programs—or even modify existing ones—without provincial consent".

The provincial finance ministers produced two demands clearly designed to limit federal powers. First, they demanded that the federal government reinstate the transfer cuts of close to $6.2 billion annually provided for health care, post-secondary education and social assistance. They also demanded $1.5 billion for equalization payments to the "have not" provinces. The second demand has serious implications for the NCBS, as the provinces are insisting that in the future the federal government negotiate and co-operate with all of the provinces on new social policy developments. Their "consensus negotiating position" is intended to prevent the federal government from unilaterally creating new programs, applying taxation to create or alter national social programs or unilaterally cutting transfer payments, as it has in the recent past.

The provinces were not unanimous on this issue. The finance minister from Newfoundland and Labrador did not endorse the plan, fearing that it would make the federal government unable to create new programs which the province itself would be unable to afford. He felt that it was in Newfoundland's best interests to maintain a strong federal government. The Québec government did not participate at all in developing the demands.

The collaborative approach proposed by the provinces would include joint setting of priorities, objectives and principles of any new national social policy initiatives. There would be sufficient flexibility to allow the provinces to adapt the program for their specific needs and guaranteed adequate, stable funding. There was also the provision to allow full funding to any province electing to opt out of the program and provide a similar program with similar objectives.

The provinces' proposal would end federal unilateralism, yet maintain the possibility of unilateral action by the provinces. Not surprisingly then, the response from the federal government was a clear rejection of any suggestion that money would transfer to the provinces without federal "strings." In addition, the federal government insisted on its right to reduce or eliminate funds as fiscal circumstances dictate.

This debate is about power. Money is both the "carrot" and the "stick" used by the federal government . Herein lies the caveat for the National Child Benefit System: If federal-provincial relations deteriorate over these and similar demands, one can expect that the program will be nothing more than a fizzle.

Defining Power: Low Income Cut-Offs

Although poverty is a commonly used word, its definition is problematic and contested. It refers to more than simply an inadequate income. Poverty is a subjective state and has subjective meanings. There are two basic orientations to defining poverty and who is poor and who is not (Ross et al. 1994:4; Oppenheim and Harker 1996:7). The first is "absolute poverty," which is defined by a minimum standard of living based on a individual's physical needs for food, clothing and shelter. Quite simply, if a person cannot supply herself with these basics, she is deemed to be living in poverty. The problem with this definition lies in how one determines "minimum" standards. It also excludes social and cultural needs (Ross et al. 1994:4; Oppenheim and Harker 1996:8).

The second definition, "relative poverty," incorporates a generally accepted standard of living in the context of the broader community at a specific time. It goes beyond biological needs to include social and cultural needs. It relates to a context shaped by culture and society; it is relative and comparative. It is comparative in that its meaning is understood by what others have—there is a lack of something within the context of what others have. It is more than a lack of material resources, but includes such concepts as social belonging, participation, empowerment and self-esteem. These two orientations form a continuum from a minimalist to a more inclusive definition of poverty (Burman 1996:19). The idea of relative poverty is not new. Adam Smith, the eighteenth-century economic philosopher, wrote in *The Wealth of Nations*:

> By necessities I understand not only commodities which are indispensably necessary for the support of life but whatever the custom of the country renders it indecent for creditable people, even of the lowest order, to be without. (Adam Smith, in Oppenheim and Harker 1996:9)

Poverty can be understood to mean when an individual or family is living in conditions without the resources to obtain food, clothing and shelter, participate in individual and social activities, or possess amenities that are commonly held by other members of the society (Oppenheim and Harker 1996:10). The ability to obtain community-held standards is dependent mainly on economic resources; hence, poverty is commonly measured using dollars as the yardstick, albeit with limitations.

There is no magical point or poverty line from which to determine who is poor and who is not poor, and most governments have resisted any attempt at an official monetized poverty line. However, various groups and organizations have developed methods to determine poverty, based upon family composition and geographic differences in the costs of necessary goods and services. For example, a family of four needs more resources than a single individual and a family living in a large urban centre needs more income resources than a family living in a rural community.

One of the most useful and recognized poverty scales is Statistics Canada's Low Income Cut-Offs (LICO). Statistics Canada does not claim to measure poverty, but rather to establish an economic threshold below which people are living in financially stressed conditions (Ross et al 1994:12). "LICO represents levels of gross income where people spend disproportionate amounts of money for food, shelter and clothing" (NCW 1998b:4). Studies have determined that in 1986 the average Canadian family spent 36.2 percent of gross income on these basic necessities. So it was determined that if an individual or family spent 20 percent more than the average family, they would be deemed to be below the cut-off. Individuals and families are considered to be living in poverty if they spend 56.2 percent of their gross income on food, shelter and clothing.

These cut-offs vary by the number of individuals in the family unit and the population of the area of residence. There is some margin of error because not all families have the same costs of necessities and not all areas are equal based population. For example, the costs of shelter are considerably different between Fort McMurray and Moose Jaw, even though they are both western communities of similar size. In addition, the expenditure of 20 percent more for basic goods and services than the average is largely arbitrary as a level of poverty. However, the LICOs have come to be respected as a logical and reasonable definition point for persons in poverty. It is worth noting that there are other scales used to describe poverty such as the Canadian Council on Social Development Income Lines, Senate Committee Poverty Lines, Metropolitan Toronto Social Planning Council Budget Guides, Montreal Diet Dispensary Guidelines and the Fraser Institute's minimalist Poverty Lines and Provincial Social Assistance Rates. For a brief description of these scales, see the CCSD publication by Ross et al (1994).

The low income cut-offs are calculated from seven categories of household size (one to seven plus) and five community sizes (rural to 500,000 plus) producing thirty-five cut-offs. Every spring, researchers at Statistics Canada complete a survey of incomes of over 34,000 households. It is important to acknowledge that their survey excludes "extreme" regions or groups, including the Yukon, the Northwest Territories, First Nations reserves and institutions such as prisons, mental health facilities, and homes for the elderly. Income refers to the monies from all family members (fifteen years or older) and includes gross wages, self-employment earnings, investment income, government payments such as federal child tax benefits, old age security and provincial tax credits, pensions

Table 1
Statistics Canada's Low Income Cut-Offs (1986 Base) for 1996

Family Size	Community Size				
	Cities of 500,000+	100,000 to 499,999	30,000 to 99,999	Less than 30,000	Rural Areas
1	16,061	14,107	13,781	12,563	10,933
2	21,769	19,123	18,680	17,027	14,823
3	27,672	24,307	23,744	21,644	18,839
4	31,862	27,982	27,338	24,922	21,690
5	34,811	30,574	29,868	27,228	23,699
6	37,787	33,185	32,420	29,554	25,724
7+	40,640	35,696	34,872	31,789	27,668

(Source: Statistics Canada 1998)

and other income from scholarships and child support payments. It does not include gambling winnings or losses, capital gains or losses, revenue from sales of property or belongings, income tax refunds, loans or insurance payments. The calculations for 1996 are presented in Table 1.

Poverty Trends

Graph 1 demonstrates a clear connection between unemployment and rates of poverty among working-age people. From 1980 to 1992, the trends between the two followed each other, rising and falling with the national economy. In the past five years, the Canadian economy grew modestly and unemployment rates declined slightly. It would be reasonable to expect that the rate of poverty would have declined. In fact, the rate of poverty actually increased to 17.6 percent of all Canadians, meaning that well over five million Canadians were living below the low income cut-off. These last few years have seen an alarming break from the previous patterns in that even though the economy has improved, the rate of poverty has increased.

Since 1980, the trend in the poverty rates of children is similar. By 1996, the child poverty rate climbed to 20.9 percent or close to 1.5 million children. Following the economic recession of 1980–81, the rate steadily rose to almost 20 percent until 1984 when it started to decline. It dipped to 14.5 percent in 1989 and there were expectations that with concerted effort it could be reduced to zero. Since the declaration to eradicate child poverty was made in 1989, the rate has increased from 14.5 percent to 20.9 percent, an overall increase of 6.4 percent or a 44.1 percent increase

Graph 1
Unemployment and Poverty among Working-Age People

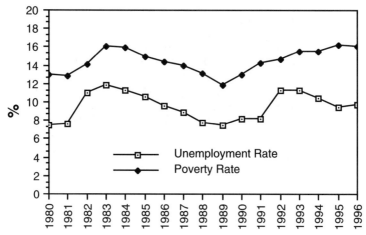

(Source: Statistics Canada 1998)

Table 2
Poverty Trends, Children under 18

Year	Number of Children Under 18 Living in Poverty	Poverty Rate %
1980	984,000	14.9
1981	998,000	15.2
1982	1,155,000	17.8
1983	1,221,000	19.0
1984	1,253,000	19.6
1985	1,165,000	18.3
1986	1,086,000	17.0
1987	1,057,000	16.6
1988	987,000	15.4
1989	934,000	14.5
1990	1,105,000	16.9
1991	1,210,000	18.3
1992	1,218,000	18.2
1993	1,415,000	20.8
1994	1,334,000	19.1
1995	1,441,000	20.5
1996	1,481,000	20.9

(Source: Statistics Canada 1998)

Graph 2
Poverty Rates for Families

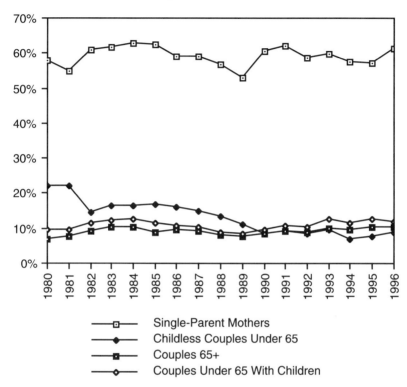

(Source: Statistics Canada 1998)

over the 1989 level! This has occurred during a time of so-called economic recovery. While many Canadians enjoyed increased prosperity, many families suffered the effects of increasing disparities.

An interesting comparison can be made between the rate of poverty in household units with and without children. Graph 2 presents poverty rates among four family types: single-parent mothers with children, couples under sixty-five with children, couples under sixty-five without children and couples sixty-five and older. The graph clearly shows the impact of dual wage earners and/or dual pensioners in reducing the overall rate of poverty. The poverty rates for couples have been relatively low and remained low regardless of the age of the couple or the presence of children.

The rate of poverty for single-parent mothers has hovered around the 60 percent mark for the past sixteen years while all other family units have remained at around 10 percent. The rate for couples over sixty-five years of age has dropped from over 22.2 percent in 1980 to 8.5 percent in 1990, where it has remained for the past six years.

Provincial Differences

Poverty rates are influenced by rates of employment, pension programs and family type, but there are also significant differences among the provinces. Table 3 represents family poverty rates and child poverty rates by province in 1996.

There were 1.2 million Canadian families in poverty in 1996, representing 14.8 percent of all families. Provincial family poverty rates range from 10.6 percent in Prince Edward Island to 17.6 percent in Québec. Sadly, there were close to 1.5 million children in these families, representing close to 21 percent of all children. Again, the children in Prince Edward Island had the lowest rate of 14.8 percent, and Manitoba had highest rate with 25.4 percent of its children in poverty.

Table 4 shows the provincial trends for two-parent families and single-parent mothers by province. As above, both couples and single-parent families in Prince Edward Island fared comparably better (8.3 percent and 45.3 percent respectively) than other provinces. Among two-parent fami-

Table 3
Poverty by Province, 1996

	Poor Children in All Family Types		Families		All Persons	
	Number of Children	Poverty Rate	Number of Poor Families	Poverty Rate	Number of Poor People	Poverty Rate %
Newfoundland	27,000	20.0%	27,000	16.6%	96,000	17.2
PEI	5,000	14.8%	4,000	10.6%	17,000	12.6
Nova Scotia	51,000	23.7%	45,000	16.4%	168,000	18.1
New Brunswick	34,000	19.6%	30,000	13.8%	119,000	15.8
Quebec	372,000	22.2%	367,000	17.6%	1,546,000	21.2
Ontario	538,000	19.9%	425,000	13.4%	1,770,000	15.8
Manitoba	69,000	25.4%	46,000	15.1%	205,000	18.8
Saskatchewan	55,000	20.9%	38,000	13.7%	161,000	16.5
Alberta	148,000	20.3%	98,000	13.1%	436,000	15.8
British Columbia	180,000	20.3%	150,000	14.3%	673,000	17.6
Canada	1,481,000	20.9%	1,230,000	14.8%	5,190,000	17.6

(Source: Statistics Canada 1998)

Table 4
Children Under 18 Living in Poverty, 1996

	Poor Children in All Family Types		Poor Children of Two-Parent Families under 65		Poor Children of Single-Parent Mothers under 65	
	Number of Children	Poverty Rate %	Number of Children	Poverty Rate %	Number of Children	Poverty Rate %
Newfoundland	27,000	20.0	15,000	12.7	11,000	72.1
PEI	5,000	14.8	2,000	8.3	2,000	45.3
Nova Scotia	51,000	23.7	25,000	14.7	24,000	70.5
New Brunswick	34,000	19.6	16,000	11.4	17,000	67.6
Quebec	372,000	22.2	184,000	13.7	167,000	62.5
Ontario	538,000	19.9	271,000	12.2	245,000	66.2
Manitoba	69,000	25.4	37,000	16.9	28,000	71.6
Saskatchewan	55,000	20.9	24,000	11.3	29,000	68.7
Alberta	148,000	20.3	69,000	11.5	72,000	70.7
British Columbia	180,000	20.3	86,000	12.0	78,000	59.8
Canada	1,481,000	20.9	730,000	12.6	673,000	65.3

(Source: Statistics Canada 1998)

lies, Manitoba stands out as the poorest of the poor (16.9 percent), and among single-parent mothers, Newfoundland is the highest with 72.1 percent in poverty.

Some interesting patterns emerge when data on the number and age of children are compared. Previous tables and graphs have shown that the poverty rates for single mothers are high and are lower for two-parent families. However, when data on the age of the children is introduced, some variances appear. Graph 3 shows that as the number of children increases so does the rate of poverty, and the rates of poverty are higher among families with young children.

Graph 4 represents similar data on poverty rates for single mothers by number and age of children. The variables of age and number of children correlate with the rate of poverty. Families with young children and three or more children have higher rates than those with only one child seven years and older. Large families with young children are more likely to find themselves below the poverty line. Single mothers with three or more children face a shocking poverty rate of 82.7 percent. The daily tasks of

Graph 3
Poverty Rates for Two-Parent Families Under 65, by Number and Age
Group of Children Under 18, 1996

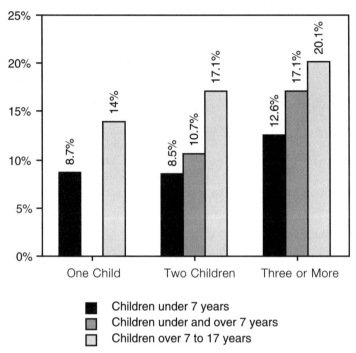

■ Children under 7 years
▨ Children under and over 7 years
☐ Children over 7 to 17 years

(Source: Statistics Canada 1998)

caring for small children and the high costs of day care keep these women out of the employment sector until their children are ready for school.

Single mothers face a rate of poverty five times greater than couples with children, a pattern that is consistent in all regions of Canada and consistent among family size and age.

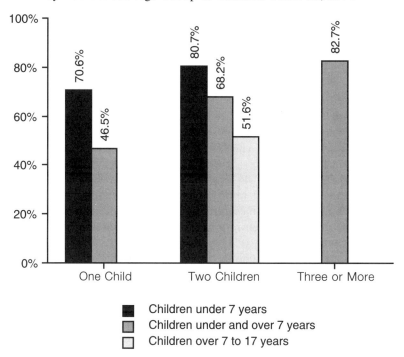

Graph 4
Poverty Rates for Single Mothers Under 65,
by Number and Age Group of Children Under 18, 1996

■ Children under 7 years
▨ Children under and over 7 years
☐ Children over 7 to 17 years

(Source: Statistics Canada 1998)

Depth of Poverty

What these tables and graphs do not show is the depth of poverty. Poverty has been defined as a low income cut-off when more than 56.2 percent of the average income is spent on necessities. These data do not show how far the individual or family rests below this cut-off. A family that is $100 below the line is much better off than a family $10,000 below the line living in the same city with the same number of children. Table 5 presents data demonstrating the increasing depth of poverty as all families slide further below the low-income cut-offs.

Two-parent and single-parent families have fallen further below the poverty line by 2.1 and 8 percent respectively. The number of these families is increasing, as is the depth of their poverty. Various social programs for seniors have protected many from poverty; however, the table demonstrates an alarming trend of an increasing depth of poverty for persons over sixty-five years of age. Single persons over sixty-five years of age living in poverty have fallen 12.4 percent from last year's levels.

25

Table 5
Increasing Depth of Poverty: Dollars Below LICOS

	1995 $	1996 $	Difference $	Percent-age
Two-parent family	9440	9634	194	2.1
Single-parent family	8637	9330	693	8.0
Unattached single over 65	2963	3331	368	12.4
All families in Canada	18.2 B	19.3 B	1.1 B	6.0

(Source: Statistics Canada 1998)

Summary

- There are close to 1.5 million Canadian children in poverty—20.9 percent of all Canadian children.
- The number of children in poverty has increased 44.1 percent from the 1989 level.
- Child poverty varies among the regions of Canada, with P.E.I. at a low of 14.8 percent, and Manitoba at a high of 25.4 percent.
- Poverty rates among working-aged people usually follow unemployment rates but have increased in recent years despite improvements in the rates of employment.
- Families with young children have higher rates of poverty.
- Families with three or more children have higher rates of poverty.
- Single mothers with three children face a rate of poverty (82.7 percent) five times greater than that of couples with children.

In Canada, poverty is increasing in all regions and all family types. Our children are not doing very well. In the wisdom of the Mohawk Nation of Kahnawake:

> We are put here by the Creator to care for each other and for Mother Earth. We should therefore be responsible for ourselves, for our families, for the next generation and for our community. (KSCS 1994:22).

The Idea of the Child and Child Rights

The following section explores some of the background to the notions of the child and child rights as they developed in North America. This context helps explain the importance of healthy child development and why child poverty is intolerable in a modern wealthy nation.

The suggestion that children are in need of protection is relatively new in Western society. The costs of reproduction and meeting the needs of children have economic consequences for all societies; community resources are consumed for the maintenance and development of children. In severe economic times all societies have resorted to measures to control the "costs" of children. Historically, "contraception and abortion, infanticide and abandonment" have been used to prevent "child welfare problems" and can be viewed in harsh economic terms as preventing the expenditure of community resources on "costly" children with problems (Kadushin and Martin 1988:35).

Attitudes and values have changed, and gradually Western society has become concerned for the welfare of dependent children. The first organized services were meant as alternatives to "infanticide and haphazard child abandonment" (Kadushin and Martin 1988:43). The development of asylums and orphanages for children were the first institutionalized child services.

The concept of childhood is socially constructed. It is culturally determined and varies from one society to another and changes over time. Prior to modern nutrition and health care, the expected lifespan was extremely brief by today's standards, often as short as thirty-five years. Maturity had to be reached early in life. The harshness of survival forced children to grow up and contribute to family income or become self-sufficient as soon as possible. Productive labour started at an early age. Often children were viewed as small adults and not seen as having preferred or special rights or entitlements.

In Western societies, a person's wealth increased along with an increase in their knowledge. Thus the process of becoming a contributing adult expanded and childhood was extended. Children were found to be "needing protection, by age segregation, and freedom from responsibilities for self-support until he or she was well into adolescence" (Kadushin and Martin 1988:55).

Still, children held the legal status of "chattel." As society began to recognize that the child held some rights, the parents were obligated to exercise their authority in the best interests of the child. In 1954, the United Nations General Assembly proclaimed the Declaration of the Rights of the Child, giving children special protections and rights, such as the right to education (Kadushin and Martin 1988:51–2). In recent decades, these rights have seen a growing acceptance: for example, the United Nations declared 1979 as the Year of the Child and in 1989, the General Assembly of the United Nations ratified the "Convention on the Rights of the Child." These rights include the right to be considered a human being (Article 1); the right to life and development (Article 6); and the child's right "to preserve his or her identity" (Article 8) (Canada 1991). The right to identity is particularly relevant to Aboriginal children and the children of recent immigrants.

These rights have developed so that "under the concept of *parens patriae,* the state has an obligation, as 'parent' to all children, to defend the rights of the child" (Kadushin and Martin 1988:219). It is this legal concept that justifies third party intervention by the state to ensure that the child's needs and rights are protected when the parent fails to meet their obligations (Zastrow 1986:165). "The justification of community intervention is based on the need for community self-preservation" (Kadushin and Martin 1988:219). The rationale for *parens patriae* did not derive from compassion or humanitarian reasons (CCCY 1978:12). Its reasons were mainly economic, allowing the state to distribute inheritances and enforce parental responsibilities of caring for their children. And herein lies the irony. While it has been a struggle for Western societies to recognize that the community needs to participate in the development of its children, this concept has historically been intimately understood and practiced by First Nations peoples in Canada and around the globe. The Mohawk people of Kahnawake have stated: "The child is sacred. Parents do not own the child. They are granted the responsibility from the Creator for raising the child, with the help of the extended family and the community" (KSCS 1994:22). Meanwhile, the media of the richest country in the world, the United States of America, celebrate Hillary Clinton's declaration of a well-known African proverb that it "takes a whole village to raise a child."

Economic Policy is Social Policy

Economic policy is social policy, as the two are inter-related and have an impact on each other. For example, if a nation enjoys a healthy and educated workforce, it has an environment that encourages and stimulates investments. There is a reason that Toyota has been expanding its operations in Cambridge, Ontario. There are cheaper places in the world to build an auto manufacturing plant and cheaper places to purchase labour. But the region in southern Ontario is rich in available women and men who are both physically and emotionally healthy and well-educated for new industrial technologies. In today's global world, a successful industrial infrastructure includes much more than simple physical labour.

Hence, poverty costs the nation, both directly and indirectly. The dimensions of poverty are wide and deep (see: CCSD 1997c; Oppenheim and Harker 1996; Walker and Walker 1997). People who are poor pay few taxes and contribute little to the general well-being of the country. Allowing children to live in poverty is short-sighted and results in serious long-term problems and costs. The costs of prevention far outweigh the costs of dealing with an uneducated, untrained and emotionally and physically unhealthy national labour force. In the end, every citizen pays the costs of poverty. This is a straightforward utilitarian argument that should appeal to those Canadians who argue for "fiscal responsibility." In the wisdom of the Mohawk Nation of Kahnawake, "When making major decisions, communities should draw on the wisdom of the past and look ahead to the effects for seven generations" (KSCS 1994:22).

Advocates Against Child and Family Poverty

This book focuses on the National Child Benefit program which has evolved from existing anti-poverty programs. The main intent of the NCB program is to reduce levels of poverty among Canada's children; therefore, it is worth identifying organizations and groups that are making significant contributions towards this goal. In recent years, these organizations have undertaken in-depth research and analysis and have produced a wealth of practical and useful information for others interested in eliminating child poverty. The major organizations involved in this goal are highlighted below. This section will be of particular interest to students, academics and policy-makers who are seeking information and data on child poverty.

It is a strange and sad contradiction that for the past five consecutive years, Canada has been ranked at the top of the United Nations' evaluation of world social development but at the bottom in terms of our rates of child poverty with only the United States and Australia lower (Hay 1997:116; UNDP 1991–98). Looking at the broader poverty picture, which includes scales of income disparities, rates of literacy, levels of long-term unemployment and other indicators, Canada rated only tenth out of seventeen industrialized countries (UNDP 1998). Although one of the richest countries in the world, Canada is plagued with significant levels of poverty. (Incidentally, the 1998 report showed the United States with the highest per capita income and worst rate of poverty (UNDP 1998)). Clearly, the many benefits Canadians enjoy are not being shared with one-fifth of the nation's children. This national embarrassment has generated a social movement of the 1990s, creating a number of advocates to eradicate child poverty. Groups such as the Canadian Council on Social Development and the Canadian Council on Children and Youth provide sustained political pressure, increased public awareness and universal support to end child poverty. In November 1989, the House of Commons unanimously passed a resolution "to seek to achieve the goal of eliminating poverty among Canadian children by the year 2000" (Canada, House of Commons 1989:6173–6228). All major political parties voiced their support for this noble and attainable goal.

Child poverty is easy to understand, and for most Canadians it is easy to declare support for its eradication; yet many people hold the notion that there are deserving and undeserving poor. In a culture that emphasizes individualism and self-sufficiency, unemployed and poor people are frequently blamed for their situation. Unlike unemployable adults, children are viewed as innocent victims of their parents' inability to provide for their needs. Hence, children in poverty are seen as deserving public support and the eradication of child poverty is viewed as a just and popular cause.

Two years after the resolution, a coalition of eighteen national partners and thirty-one provincial and community organizations was formed, declaring, "we are committed to promoting and securing the full implementation of the House of Commons Resolution" to eliminate child poverty by the year 2000 (Hay 1997:117). They called themselves, simply, "Campaign 2000." Since November 1991, they have lobbied to keep the issue of child poverty on the public and political agenda. Their activities have included the preparation and presentation of briefs to federal committees, commissions and task forces, the organization of education and awareness meetings with members of Parliament, and the support and education of local partners and related groups. Each year, the campaign produces their annual report, *Child Poverty in Canada,* summarizing the poverty conditions of children and families. Member organizations also release reports, deliver education and awareness events and lobby provincial politicians for improved social welfare programs for children (Hay 1997:118).

In the United Kingdom, the Child Poverty Action Group has been the voice against the growth of child and family poverty for over thirty years. Their book, *Poverty, the Facts,* succinctly presents the extent of poverty, its causes and its impacts on women and people of colour (Oppenheim and Harker 1996). They have campaigned tirelessly for social policies for low income families, "in order to eradicate the injustice of poverty" (Oppenheim and Harker 1996:ii). In Canada, a group with the same name has also being advocating out of Ontario and since 1986 they have published several reports.

Another prominent advocate for children is the National Anti-Poverty Organization (NAPO). This national coalition of grassroots groups has taken a firm position rejecting the "tinkering" approach to poverty and has called for a national strategy to deal with all poverty. They argue for decent jobs with decent wages and adequate welfare benefits for those unable to work. They have criticized poverty policies such as the NCB as suppressing wages and forcing the poor into low-wage employment. As they say, "child poverty is related to all poverty" (NAPO 1998:3).

The National Council of Welfare (NCW) is an important and respected contributor to the dissemination of information on poverty issues. It was "established by the Government Organization Act, 1969, as a citizens' advisory body to the federal government" (NCW 1998b:97). Although an independent body, it has been created to provide information relating to poverty and low-income people to the Minister of Human Resources Development. The NCW is comprised of members who represent the regions of Canada and are appointed by the Governor-in-Council. Acting in their capacities as private individuals, the members come from diverse backgrounds and include social assistance recipients, the working poor, and social and community workers and educators. The council regularly produces informative reports on poverty and social welfare policy which are available through government and public libraries. Drawing on Statistics Canada information, their reports are an important source of data for community advocacy groups and organizations.

The Canadian Council on Social Development (CCSD) promotes the improvement of economic and social security for Canadians. It is a national, self-supporting, non-profit organization created to conduct social research and produce accessible information on poverty, child welfare, income security, employment, pensions and related social policy issues (CCSD 1997c).

The Caledon Institute of Social Policy regularly releases valuable reports and summaries of poverty and its impact on Canadians. Other groups working on the issue include the Child Welfare League of Canada, the various Children's Aid Associations, the Canadian Association of Social Workers and the Canadian Teacher's Federation. Students, researchers and policy makers will find that many of these organizations have web sites and can easily be accessed for valuable information. In addition, Statistics Canada has a direct route to its data information, including the 1996 census, and can be located at www.statscan.ca.

Full Circle: Background to the Family Allowance

The family allowance program was a mainstay of the Canadian social welfare scene for almost fifty years. The "baby-bonus" has been a way of life for many families in every region of Canada. In 1949, the program's social and economic benefits were included in the debate in favour of confederation for Newfoundlanders. Today, the family allowance program is history and the present generation of families has little knowledge of its roots and the role it played in shaping the Canadian social welfare system. However, its legacy has shaped Canada's new National Child Benefit program and the debates and arguments of the family allowance program are being echoed in the discussion of this new program. In some ways, the debates have come full circle.

31

Prior to the 1920s, a number of European countries boasted various family allowance schemes. These plans generated some interest in North America but the general feeling was that the wages in Canada and the United States were sufficient to support a family (Kitchen 1987:222). The connection between the inadequacy of wages and family needs was central to the rationale for these European programs and the argument for a similar program in Canada, where it was argued that it was unfair that a wage-earner with a large family had to meet its needs under a wage scale that was based on the needs of an individual. The supplementary financial support of a family allowance was to address this inequity (Kitchen 1987:222). However, in Europe, there were other social reasons for family allowances. For example, it was believed that these programs would stimulate a declining birthrate or prevent emigration of labour to neighbouring countries where better wages or employment opportunities existed.

In Canada, the one of the earliest proponents of family allowances was the Jesuit priest, Father Leon Lebel. This father of family allowances (pun intended) wrote a number of pamphlets about the financial difficulties faced by large families (Kitchen 1987:224). He recognized that industrialization caused structural changes in the economic system, resulting in the failure to provide for large families. His arguments were based on the principles of justice and fairness and acknowledged the cost of raising children (Kitchen 1987:225). Reproduction and population growth benefited all members of society and the costs should be shared equally. Therefore, family allowance should be provided regardless of employment status; whether or not one is working should not be a determinant of eligibility.

Hence family allowances were seen not as a disincentive to work, but a recognition of reproduction costs, the service of raising children for society. Parenthood was a social service to the nation and should be supported by all.

In 1929, the House of Commons established a Select Standing Committee to examine insurance for the unemployed, the sick and the disabled, and part of their discussions explored family allowances. Lebel appeared before the committee and portrayed the declining birthrate as a national concern; support for families therefore had an important social function—to maintain the population and ensure continued economic and social growth (Kitchen 1987:228). Others, particularly social workers, argued against the family allowance program because they felt it would erode the responsibility of each individual to provide for his or her family. They also feared a stimulated birthrate would tax other resources, placing greater demands on services. In addition, from the perspective of these early social workers, large families were not to be encouraged, because they were the major source of a variety of social problems like poverty and juvenile crime (Kitchen 1987:230). While the argument about the inability of current wages to support a family were compelling, the discussion faded with the stock market crash of 1929 and the beginning of the Great Depression.

In 1943, Dr. Leonard Marsh released his now respected *Report on Social Security for Canada,* outlining a comprehensive Canadian social security system. He recommended that an unemployment and health insurance program be a priority and be established before a family allowance program. His report fell into the shadow of the historic British document of 1942, *Social Insurance and Allied Services* by Sir William Beveridge. Marsh's recommendation was ignored and the report was not popular in federal government circles (Kitchen 1987:234).

Ursel presents the argument that the creation of the family allowance was primarily to subsidize wages to control the demand for increases in wages (1992:190). During the war, the federal government enacted The War Measures Act to control wages. Prior to the war, the Depression created high unemployment and the war stimulated the economy. During war, the economy heated up, creating a demand for labour while Canadian men enlisted, effectively removing themselves from the labour pool. There was pressure to increase wages, thereby enticing men to not enlist. After years of unemployment, many workers could find good paying jobs. Thus, inflation would make the costs of war even higher. The War Measures Act could control wages and contain the costs of the war effort (Ursel 1992:190).

It was generally believed by government leaders and bureaucrats that after the war there would be stagnation in the economy and the return of an economic depression, but this did not occur (McGilly 1998: 153; Ursel 1992:190). In the midst of the Second World War, the debate for a family allowance rested on two competing perspectives: one to support family incomes and the other to suppress wages.

With end of the war in sight, labour was creating pressure to lift wage controls. "The driving force behind the development of the Family Allowances program was the stalemate between business and labour over wages" (Ursel 1992: 191). Finance documents reported that "children's allowances are the most direct and economic method of meeting the current strong demand for relaxation of wage control in respect of the lower wage rates. If current dissatisfaction of lower-paid workers is met by allowing them unrestricted wage bargaining (and thus promoting union organization) a good deal of industrial strife and stoppage of essential work must be expected" (Finance Files, June 14, 1943 in Ursel 1992:195)

Not wanting to link these two issues in the public debate, there was a deliberate move by federal authorities to separate the issues. Ursel (1992) presents government memos that direct officials to keep documents and reports that discussed the issues of wage restraints and family allowances separate. Prime Minister King and his senior advisors "were well aware that family allowances would have to be kept separate from any discussion on labour policy and would have to be considered in relation to social security coverage" (Kitchen 1987:235).

> Prominence and emphasis was given to Keynesian economic principles which considered family allowances as a sure and valuable economic primer which would stimulate the economy through increasing the spending capacity of those Canadians with the highest "propensity" for consumption, i.e. low-income families. This would prevent a post-war economic recession. (Kitchen 1987:236).

However, "family allowances were argued for, not only as a means of rescuing the wage stabilization program and restoring industrial harmony, but also as a basis of developing a competitive post-war economy" (Ursel 1992:195).

In a strange irony that could just as well be heard today, Finance documents record, "Children's allowances are likely to protect Canada's ability to compete with other counties in world markets. In the long run, minimum wages and average wages are likely to be pushed higher in the absence of family allowances than they would be if this supplementary equalization measure were in effect" (Finance Files, June 14, 1943 in Ursel 1992:195).

The purpose of the equalizing effect of family allowances was not justice or recognition of the costs of reproduction, but to support wage controls, maintain "industrial harmony" by discouraging collective bargaining, and support economic competitiveness in the world economy. The public argument for family allowances was different and was based on the inadequacy of current wages to support families. The 1941 census found that of all gainfully employed people 48 percent were single and 20 percent were married or widowed with no children. The census showed that 19 percent of the employed supported 84 percent of the dependent children (Ursel 1992:196). Thought was given to placing an income ceiling and targeting the benefits to the lower income families, but such a ceiling "would save little; a ceiling of $3000 would exclude only 3 percent of all families" (Finance Files, September, 1943 in Ursel 1992:196). As a result, the program was presented as universal, for all children regardless of family income.

Family allowances, it was argued, would contribute to economic and political stability after the war. "Dr Marsh felt that family allowances should meet the basic subsistence needs of the child" (Ursel 1992:238). In a sense, the plan was the first proposed guaranteed income. However, the 1944 Act failed to offer a serious minimum for all children and appeared only as a contribution to the costs of raising a child—a supplement to the family.

As a new social welfare program, the family allowance was unique for a number of reasons. First, the recipients of the program never asked for it. Canadians were busy with the war and few had ever even thought of such a plan. Second, "although it was destined to become a critical component of the modern welfare state, welfare commissions, inquiries and department had nothing to do with its development" (Ursel 1992:190). It was created in isolation from normal social program development. Third, its proponents were an unlikely group to create a national universal social program. The architects were senior bureaucrats in the Departments of External Affairs and Finance and the Governor of the Bank of Canada. These people had been extremely influential in managing the war economy and represented Canada's business elite (Ursel 1992:191).

When the program was announced, public opinion was rather flat. Labour argued that it would suppress wages, but soon found their criticisms were unpopular with the public. Among the political parties, both the Conservatives and the CCF eventually endorsed the program. As it turned out, there were few who strongly opposed or supported it and the political and public debates fizzled (Ursel 1992:197).

Ursel's analysis is interesting, as she states that "the family allowance scheme was the most direct form of state mediation of production and reproduction" (1992:197). It was a compromise between labour and business that subsidized wages, ignoring reproductive costs (Ursel 1992:198). "The history of the initiation of family allowances permits us to peek behind the disguise and see the essential purpose of the welfare state, the mediation of these two contradictory spheres"—the contradiction between production and reproduction (Ursel 1992:198).

Interestingly, Ursel writes the following in the dying days of the program: "But as long as the wage system fails to provide families with horizontal equity and the tax system does not provide vertical equity, the case for family allowances remains strong and unshakable" (Ursel 1992:239). The program ceased in 1993.

The family allowance program provided benefits of a monthly average of $5.94 per child and $14.18 per family in 1946. The amount was far below Marsh's recommendation of $7.50 per child (Guest 1980:132). Over the years, the benefits were steadily increased and in 1985 the monthly benefits averaged $31 per child. There were numerous minor changes over the fifty years and, within limits, the provinces could change the patterns of benefits. Québec established its own system in 1967 (McGilly 1990:178).

The federal government initiated the Child Tax Credit program re-placing child deductions in income tax in 1988. For a few years, families received a family allowance of $31 per month per child and low income families received a tax credit of $384 per year, making a total benefit of $750 per year per child. This sum represents about one-quarter of the Senate committee's poverty line for maintaining a child (Armitage 1996:78). During these years there were some minor variations between the prov-inces.

The tax credit was designed to accommodate the contradictory nature of the progressive income tax structure and the way that tax deductions impact on the amount of tax payable. The switch to tax credits from income tax deductions was significant for many Canadians. A tax credit of $1,000 is of equal value to both low and high taxpayers. But, a deduction of $1,000 has greater benefit for the higher income earner. The higher taxpayer is paying a higher percentage of income as taxes and a $1,000 deduction means a greater savings in taxes than it does for a lower income earner. Someone who pays no income tax sees no benefit. For example, a taxpayer at a 20 percent tax level receives a $200 benefit, while a taxpayer at a 50 percent tax bracket enjoys a $500 benefit.

A tax credit is a method for income redistribution, intended to address the inequities that favoured the higher income earners. It has become Canada's primary technique for income redistribution (McGilly 1998:153).

In 1993, family allowances and the new Child Tax Credit were re-placed by the Child Tax Benefit and Working Income Supplement (McGilly 1998:153). The termination of the family allowance brought to an end the last social welfare program based on the principle of universality.

Today, the federal Child Tax Benefit and other family benefits consti-tute a substantial portion of the incomes of low-income families, includ-ing the working poor. The refundable Child Tax Benefit is the largest and best known of the redistributive tax credits. It provides a cash benefit for persons with dependent children through the income tax system (McGilly 1998:154) and it benefits low-income earners who depend upon low-paying, part-time or seasonal labour and social assistance.

Those individuals who have earned sufficient family net income to pay taxes receive a tax credit and have their taxes reduced by the amount of the benefit. The credit is paid up to an income threshold. Beyond the threshold, the tax credit is gradually reduced until, at a family income slightly above the national average, it is reduced to zero (McGilly 1998:154). The threshold has been raised, but less than the rate of inflation, thereby decreasing the real value of the benefit.

If the taxpayer's income is sufficiently low that he/she does not owe any tax, then a cash benefit is paid. This is why it is called a refundable tax credit; the tax credit is paid regardless of the amount of tax due. The benefit is paid in the form of a monthly cheque or bank account deposit (McGilly 1998:155).

Parents with direct expenses for child care, incurred for employment, can deduct these from their income for tax purposes. These deductions take advantage of the progressive nature of the income structure, thereby benefiting higher income earners.

After close to fifty years, the family allowance program and its universality has drawn to close. In the following chapters, the authors explain, explore and debate its replacement with the National Child Benefit program, just as Lebel, Marsh and others debated the family allowance program some half a century ago.

2

The National Child Benefit:
Best Thing Since Medicare
or New Poor Law?

Ken Battle

The National Child Benefit announced in the 1997 federal budget pro-
voked three kinds of responses from social policy groups and children's
advocates: negative—"seriously flawed method of enriching incomes for
poor children ... victimizing the poorest" (Pulkingham, Ternowetsky and
Hay 1997:6); guarded support—"A small step forward ... the overall
thrust of the reforms proposed by the federal, provincial and territorial
governments is promising" (NCW 1997:12); and guarded enthusiasm—
"has the potential to be the most important social policy innovation
since medicare. But the 1997 federal budget is only a down payment ...
Much work remains to be done, by both levels of government, individu-
ally and together." (Caledon Institute of Social Policy 1997:1). The media and general public, for the most part, appeared indifferent to the
initiative.

The negative or wary reaction of the non-governmental social policy
community to the 1997 federal budget's child benefit changes was under-
standable and predictable. Any major social policy initiative is bound to
spark controversy, especially when it involves the welfare system. But
there are a number of reasons why social advocates are particularly leery
of governments bearing social policy gifts in the 1990s.

Welfare recipients and welfare rights groups feel vulnerable to welfare bashing, which is more evident than ever these days. Welfare has
been the subject of benefit cuts or freezes and other forms of constraint in
virtually every province in recent years, most prominently in Alberta and
Ontario. The Conservative government of Mike Harris campaigned on a
get-tough-with-welfare platform in Ontario and followed through with a
huge (21.6 percent) cut in welfare benefits for most recipients, the impo-
sition of work-for-welfare and bolstered anti-fraud measures.

After a decade and a half of both overt and stealthy changes to
virtually every major federal and provincial social program, social advocates have every right to be suspicious of "reform." Most—but not all—of
the social program changes have been regressive. The changes made to

federal social transfers to the provinces, unemployment insurance (recently renamed employment insurance), the Canada Pension Plan, the income tax system, the refundable GST credit, welfare and social services generally weigh heaviest on low-income families and individuals. The numerous cuts that governments have made to social programs—in relatively few years profoundly altering and in some cases weakening the social infrastructure that took decades to build—are all the harder to swallow when contrasted to the historic 1989 Commons resolution against child poverty.

The dismal trend in the poverty statistics also has made a mockery of the 1989 resolution. The percentage of children in low-income families has increased from 15.3 percent in 1989 (one child in seven) to 21.1 percent in 1996 (one child in five), the most recent year for which income data are available. Six in ten children (61.9 percent) in single-parent families led by women lived on low incomes at last count compared with one in seven (13 percent) children in two-parent families (Statistics Canada 1997c:32–37). Since 1989, the number of low-income children has increased by close to half a million (482,000) or by 47 percent (from 1,016,000 in 1989 to 1,498,000 in 1996). More troubling still, 1995 was the first year that the poverty rate did not decrease despite falling unemployment, rising GDP and substantial employment creation; 1996 brought no respite in poverty despite growth in jobs and the economy (Battle 1997).

It is worth pointing out that the 1989 resolution is typically misquoted by the media and social groups to say that the federal government committed itself "to end child poverty by the year 2000." That is not the case. The actual wording contained a not insignificant qualifier—"*to seek* to achieve the goal of eliminating poverty among Canadian children by the year 2000."

Until recently, Ottawa and the provinces have not done much "seeking" after child poverty, though the federal government would argue that its successful campaign to eliminate the deficit is a prerequisite to any campaign against child poverty. However, developments over the past few years—politically jump-started by the provinces' Ministerial Council on Social Policy Reform and Renewal and culminating in the 1997 federal budget announcement of a redesign of federal child benefits and related joint federal-provincial efforts to create a National Child Benefit—mark the first potentially positive social policy initiative against child poverty in many years.

The main purpose of this chapter is to contribute to the public debate on the National Child Benefit by summarizing and discussing criticisms which social groups have levelled against the initiative. First, however, I briefly describe the child benefit changes announced in the 1997 federal budget and then explain why the Caledon Institute considers the National Child Benefit to have the potential to become a major advance in Canadian social policy.

The 1997 Federal Budget and the National Child Benefit

The 1997 federal budget contained two major announcements on child benefits involving joint action on the part of the federal and provincial governments. The federal government will increase and reconfigure the Child Tax Benefit as the Canada Child Tax Benefit. The provinces will reallocate savings from welfare expenditures for children, made possible by the increase in federal child benefits, to various other programs and services for low-income families with children. The federal Canada Child Tax Benefit and provincial reinvestment in programs for low-income families with children in combination will form what Ottawa and the provinces formally have termed the "National Child Benefit System" (more commonly known as the National Child Benefit).

The federal changes are being phased in over two years. In 1997, Ottawa shifted the Working Income Supplement from its current annual maximum of $500 per family to a per-child benefit worth a maximum of $605 for the first child, $405 for the second child and $330 for the third and each additional child. The Working Income Supplement is a special benefit introduced as part of the Child Tax Benefit when the latter program replaced family allowances and the refundable and non-refundable child tax credits in 1993; the Working Income Supplement phases in when earnings reach $3,750, pays its maximum benefit between $10,000 and $20,921 and phases out once net family income reaches $25,921. Including the current Child Tax Benefit, in 1997 total federal child benefits for working poor families increased to $1,625 for one child and $1,425 for the second and each additional child, plus the existing $213 supplement for each child under seven for whom child care expenses are not claimed. Federal child benefits for other low-income families (i.e., families on welfare and EI) in 1997 remained at a maximum $1,020 per child plus the existing $213 young-child supplement and $75 supplement for the third and each additional child. According to the federal government, the changes to the Working Income Supplement increased costs by $195 million and benefitted 720,000 families or 23 percent of the 3.2 million families that receive the Child Tax Benefit (Department of Finance Canada 1997:16).

In 1998, the Working Income Supplement is being absorbed into a larger and simplified Canada Child Tax Benefit paying all low-income families—whatever combination of income they receive from wages, welfare, employment insurance and other sources—a maximum $1,625 for the first child and $1,425 for each additional child, augmented by the existing $213 supplement for children under seven for whom child care expenses are not claimed. In other words, the federal child benefits provided to working poor families in 1997 are being extended to all low-income families in 1998. The 1998 changes add another $655 million to the federal child benefits budget and increase payments to an estimated 1.4 million families (44 percent of Child Tax Benefit families) with 2.5 million children (44 percent of the 5.7 million children for whom the Child Tax Benefit is paid) (Department of Finance Canada 1997:18).

The new Canada Child Tax Benefit will use a lower threshold for maximum payments (net family income of $20,921 as opposed to the current $25,921) and a higher reduction rate between net family income of $20,921 and $25,921 in order to focus benefit increases on families with net incomes below $25,921. However, families with net incomes above $25,921 will continue to receive the same benefits as they do now. The Canada Child Tax Benefit, like the Child Tax Benefit, which it replaces, will provide partial benefits to most non-poor families. Benefits disappear at relatively high incomes—e.g., net family income of $75,241 for families with one child under seven, $70,981 for families with one child under and one child over seven, $66,721 for two children over seven, and $101,401 for families with three children under seven.

The changes are summarized in Table 1. All low-income families receive more federal child benefits in 1998 than they did in 1996, though the increases vary according to the number of children and whether or not the family used to receive the Working Income Supplement (i.e., was working poor). The gains are smaller for working poor than other low-income families because the former received more federal child benefits from the old system (i.e., the Working Income Supplement in addition to the basic Child Tax Benefit). The gains for working poor families increase according to the number of children because the Working Income Supplement favoured small families (since it was a per-family rather than per-child benefit). The opposite is the case for other low-income families because the Canada Child Tax Benefit pays a larger benefit for the first child.

The changes to federal child benefits are one part of the National Child Benefit System. The federal Canada Child Tax Benefit will provide a stronger and level foundation upon which the provinces can build in varying ways. Provinces will deduct the increases in federal child benefits from welfare payments on behalf of children, but they must reinvest these savings in other programs for low-income families with children, such as income-tested child benefits, wage supplements, in-kind benefits (e.g., supplementary health care) and social services (e.g., child care). Together, the Canada Child Tax Benefit and the provincial reinvestments will constitute the National Child Benefit System.

Table 1
Maximum Federal Child Benefits, Working Poor and
Other Low-Income Families, by Number of Children,[1] 1996–1998

Working Poor Families[2]	1996 $	1997 $	1998 $	1996/98 $	1996/98 %
1 child	1,520	1,625	1,625	105	6.9
2 children	2,540	3,050	3,050	510	20.1
3 children	3,635	4,475	4,475	840	23.1
4 children	4,730	5,900	5,900	1,170	24.7
Other low-income families[3]	1996 $	1997 $	1998 $	1996/98 $	1996/98 %
1 child	1,020	1,020	1,625	605	59.3
2 children	2,040	2,040	3,050	1,010	49.5
3 children	3,135	3,135	4,475	1,340	42.7
4 children	4,230	4,230	5,900	1,670	39.5

1. add $213 for each child under 7 for whom child care expenses are not claimed
2. includes Working Income Supplement in 1996 and 1997
3. includes working poor and low-income families on Employment Insurance

(Sources: Department of Finance Canada; Caledon Institute of Social Policy)

The 1998 Federal Budget and the National Child Benefit

The 1998 federal budget announced a second $850 million increase to the Canada Child Tax Benefit, to be phased in, half by July 1999 and half by July 2000. However, the details of the design of this second phase of the Canada Child Tax Benefit were being worked out at the time of writing and were to be made public in the 1999 federal budget.

Caledon's Vision of a National Child Benefit

The Caledon Institute of Social Policy's vision of an effective child benefit goes well beyond the changes announced in the 1997 budget, which are just the first stage in the development of the National Child Benefit System. If the federal and provincial governments went no farther than the changes announced in the budget, we would view them as a

42

worthy but limited advance in social policy. We characterized the budget's child benefits changes as "having the potential to be the most important social policy innovation since medicare" because they launch what promises to be a major structural reform of both the child benefit and welfare systems (Caledon Institute of Social Policy 1997:1).

The 1997 federal budget paper (Canada 1997b), *Working Together Towards a National Child Benefit System*, speaks of the "welfare wall" as one of the key deficiencies of the current child benefits system. The "welfare wall," a concept coined by the Caledon Institute of Social Policy in 1993, referred in its initial usage to the fact that welfare recipients face a wall of high marginal tax rates if they try to supplement their social assistance benefits with outside earnings—the main (though not only) factor being the high welfare taxback which reduces benefits dollar for dollar of earnings above a relatively low level of exempt earnings.

Caledon went on to extend the concept of the welfare wall to the child benefits system. In most provinces, welfare families with children receive about twice as much in child benefits as other low-income families not on welfare, namely the working poor and families receiving employment insurance. Welfare families receive child benefits from two levels of government—the federal Child Tax Benefit and provincial welfare benefits payable on behalf of children. Working poor (and middle-income) families receive only federal child benefits—the basic Child Tax Benefit and, if families have low earnings, the Working Income Supplement.

In an example given in the 1997 federal budget paper, a prototypical welfare family with two children (one under and one over seven) gets almost twice as much total child benefits ($5,253) as a working poor family with two children ($2,753). There are real-life examples as well. In B.C., before the B.C. Family Bonus was created in 1996, a welfare family with two children seven and eleven got $4,512 ($2,040 from the Child Tax Benefit and $2,472 from B.C.'s welfare system) as opposed to the maximum $2,540 in federal child benefits for a working poor family.

If a parent leaves welfare for the workforce, she will lose thousands of dollars in cash and in-kind child benefits; face employment-related expenses (e.g., clothing for work, transportation and child care); and will have her (likely already low) wages reduced by Canada Pension Plan contributions, employment insurance premiums and federal (and, in many provinces, provincial) income taxes. Provincial child benefits provided by the welfare system constitute part of the welfare wall, which exacerbates other major problems such as the lack of affordable child care and decent jobs, that make it hard for many families with children to escape welfare.

The solution to this problem is an integrated child benefit, meaning a common child benefit paid to all low-income families by a program that is separate from the welfare system. British Columbia was the first jurisdiction to create an integrated child benefit when, in July of 1996, it replaced welfare benefits for children with the B.C. Family Bonus—an income-tested program delivered by Revenue Canada on behalf of B.C. that serves low-income and modest-income families with children in the province. Saskatchewan and Québec also are introducing integrated child benefit programs.

Caledon views an integrated child benefit as a fundamental advance in social policy. Not only would an integrated child benefit correct the present unequal treatment of poor children depending upon their parents' major source of income, it also would lay the foundation for a form of guaranteed income for children, which could be achieved by boosting the level of maximum child benefits from the federal Canada Child Tax Benefit and supplementing that amount with provincial income-tested child benefits. All low-income families with children throughout Canada would receive the same amount in federal child benefits from a broadly based income-tested system that also provides payments to the majority of non-poor families with children.

Let me make perfectly clear that Caledon does not view an integrated child benefit as the final answer to child poverty. Poverty is a complex problem that is deeply rooted in our economy and society; children are poor because their parents are poor, and their parents are poor for any number of reasons. Child poverty cannot be vanquished by a magic bullet. Indeed, we titled our January 1995 report which proposed and costed an integrated child benefit *One Way to Fight Child Poverty* to make the point that child poverty must be tackled on a number of fronts using a wide range of public and private interventions (Battle and Muszynski 1995). These include social, employment and health programs; fiscal and monetary policy; family-friendly workplace practices, parental leave and leave for family responsibilities; and community-based initiatives. However, income security programs such as child benefits greatly reduce poverty and income inequality, and could do a lot more to combat child poverty— as evidenced by the more successful efforts of most European countries.

Caledon has fleshed out its vision of an integrated child benefit to include the following requirements:

- There should be broadly based, income-tested monthly cash child benefit serving low-income and middle-income families with children.
- The maximum benefit should be payable to all low-income families regardless of their source(s) of income, with diminishing payments to non-poor families.
- Maximum benefit should increase during the first stage to a level sufficient to replace welfare benefits for children (around $2,500 per

child) by the year 2000. Further increases in the maximum benefit are required after 2000 to reach (by 2010 at the latest) the goal of covering the cost of raising a child for low-income families. We have proposed a maximum Canada Child Tax Benefit of at least $4,000 per child as a target level for this second stage of the National Child Benefit.

- The Canada Child Tax Benefit and provincial income-tested child benefits and employment earnings supplements should be fully indexed to the cost of living (both benefits and income thresholds for maximum payments).
- Over time, the Canada Child Tax Benefit should gradually improve benefits for non-poor families, beginning with modest-income families (e.g., $25,921–$35,000).
- The Canada Child Tax Benefit and provincial income-tested child benefits should use gross family income to calculate eligibility for and amount of benefits instead of the current net family income definition (because net income allows well-off families to reduce their income through regressive tax deductions and thus qualify for substantially more child benefits than their actual income would permit).
- Provinces can choose to vary the Canada Child Tax Benefit according to age and/or rank of child (within federally established limits) and can provide their own income-tested child benefits and/or employment earnings supplements on top of the federal national base.
- Both levels of government must make publicly available detailed data, evaluation results and other information required for social groups and non-governmental experts to independently monitor and evaluate progress and should create an institutional mechanism whereby such groups' views can be made known to policy-makers, administrators and the media.

Criticisms of the National Child Benefit

The National Child Benefit has been criticized vigorously by social advocacy and research groups. Their major allegations are discussed below. Of course, every group does not necessarily level all the criticisms mentioned.

1. The National Child Benefit is unfair to the working poor

Critics were quick to point out that families with one child will be $395 worse off under the Canada Child Tax Benefit than they would have been under the 1996 budget proposal to double the Working Income Supplement (from $500 to $1,000), and those with two children will get only a small ($10) increase.

45

This criticism often fails to specify that it is only one-child *working poor* families which qualify for the Working Income Supplement—not "families with one child" (i.e., not those on welfare or employment insurance)—and thus will get less from the Canada Child Tax Benefit than if the 1996 plan to double the Working Income Supplement had gone ahead. Only 289,000 or 8.7 percent of all Child Tax Benefit families receive the maximum Working Income Supplement, so by my estimate only around 120,000 families or 3.6 percent of the 3.3 million families with the Child Tax Benefit will lose the full $395. Moreover, families that receive a partial Working Income Supplement will lose less than $395. Overall, of the 792,000 families which receive the Working Income Supplement, an estimated 330,000 or 10 percent of all Child Tax Benefit families have one child and so will get less from the Canada Child Tax Benefit than they would have if Ottawa had kept to its original plan to double the Working Income Supplement.

But such numbers are beside the point in any case. This criticism is based on a fundamental misunderstanding of what Ottawa and the provinces are trying to accomplish with the National Child Benefit. The criticism treats the Canada Child Tax Benefit as if it were still the Child Tax Benefit. The aim of the Canada Child Tax Benefit is to increase federal child benefits for all low-income families—not just the working poor—to displace and eventually (given adequate increases in future) to fully replace welfare benefits for children. Moreover, some if not all working poor families under the National Child Benefit also will become eligible for provincial child-related benefits (as is the case with B.C.'s Family Bonus) in the form of cash and/or services.

This criticism is ironic in view of the fact that social groups opposed the Working Income Supplement when it was introduced in 1993 as part of the new Child Tax Benefit on the grounds that it discriminated against poor families not in the workforce. The 1997 budget will do away with the very benefit that advocacy groups criticized four years previously—and that they now use to fault Ottawa for not doubling.

The Working Income Supplement is one of the shortcomings of the existing child benefits system. The Working Income Supplement does not really live up to its billing as a work incentive and earnings supplementation program for the working poor.

The Working Income Supplement favours small families because, unlike the Child Tax Benefit and welfare, it does not adjust for the number of children in a family. Its per-family rather than per-child benefit structure and modest payment (a maximum $500 per family) mean that the Working Income Supplement does little to compensate for the loss of welfare benefits for children in the case of parents who move from welfare to work. Because the Working Income Supplement remains at its maximum amount for family earnings between $10,000 and $20,000, it does not reward increases in employment earnings in this wide range. The Working Income Supplement is a relatively blunt instrument that does not take account of differences in provinces' welfare and other income programs and in their family income distributions.

The Working Income Supplement's main shortcoming is that it is "invisible." Its recipients do not know that part of their federal child benefit is meant to reward their work effort because the Working Income Supplement is submerged in the total Child Tax Benefit payment. Nor is the Working Income Supplement responsive to changes in earnings because of the long lag (up to eighteen months) between assessment of a family's income and payment; the Child Tax Benefit suffers from the same problem of lack of responsiveness to income changes.

2. The National Child Benefit is unfair to welfare families with children

This is by far the most serious and damning criticism of the National Child Benefit. It has taken various forms, paraphrased below (note that I am describing the criticisms, not subscribing to them).

- Welfare families—the poorest of the poor, representing the majority (60 percent) of low-income families with children—will receive no increase because the provinces will be allowed to deduct increased federal child benefits from welfare benefits paid on behalf of children.

- By increasing child benefits for the working poor (through larger federal benefits and reinvestment in provincial programs for the working poor), governments are implying that working poor families with children deserve additional help while welfare families with children do not.

- Welfare families will be worse off because the National Child Benefit will be financed by cuts to welfare, as the B.C. government did when it helped finance its new B.C. Family Bonus from reductions in welfare benefits for some adults and the elimination of the provincial sales tax credit for children.

- The National Child Benefit will exacerbate the current mood of welfare bashing by favouring the working poor and accentuating the distinction between the "undeserving" welfare poor and the "deserving" working poor.

- Welfare families should not trust an integrated child benefit, which can be cut at the whim of governments.

- The real purpose behind the National Child Benefit is to reduce the welfare rolls, which is punitive to welfare families and in any case naive because the real problem is not the welfare wall but the lack of jobs on the other side and decent child care services.

Before discussing these criticisms, it is important to understand that all low-income families with children—those on welfare included—will receive the new Canada Child Tax Benefit. Some critics contend erroneously that the Canada Child Tax Benefit will be restricted to the working poor. For instance, the Canadian Council on Social Development's report *The Progress of Canada's Children 1997* claims that the Canada Child Tax Benefit "will provide financial assistance to low- and modest-income, wage-earning families on a sliding scale, depending upon their earnings" (CCSD 1997a:55). In fact, the Canada Child Tax Benefit will serve low-income, modest-income and middle-income families; the amount of benefit varies according to net family income, not earnings from wages; and the source of that income is irrelevant, so the new program will serve families without wages (e.g., families on social benefits such as welfare or employment insurance) as well as those with earnings from employment and self-employment.

It is true that, in this first stage, the National Child Benefit will not increase child benefits for welfare families and will augment child benefits only for low-income families not on welfare (i.e., working poor and low-income employment insurance families). But the federal and provincial governments justify this differential treatment as necessary to provide non-welfare families child benefits equivalent to those on welfare, who currently receive substantially more child benefits (income and in-kind). The basic objective of an integrated child benefit is to end the distinction between welfare children and other low-income children by treating welfare families the same for child benefit purposes as working poor families—and by delivering their child benefits outside of welfare. In other words, an integrated child benefit treats all low-income families with children equally.

On a point of fact, it is not the case that 60 percent of low-income families rely mainly on welfare. The National Council of Welfare, using Statistics Canada's Survey of Consumer Finances, found that only 29.6 percent of families with children rely on welfare alone—less than the 31.5 percent of families with children who count employment earnings as their main source of income. Overall, about half of low-income families with children have some connection with the labour force; they either receive employment insurance or are working (NCW 1998b).

At this stage in the development of the National Child Benefit, governments have chosen to devote their resources to reducing the child benefits differential between welfare families and other low-income families. Critics of this approach must believe either of two things; it would help the public debate if they made their views known on this crucial point. On the one hand, they may believe that welfare families deserve larger child benefits than the working poor and low-income families on employment insurance (presumably because they consider welfare families to be the poorest of the poor). Alternatively, they may feel that all low-income families should get the same child benefits, but that those on welfare should get more than they do now given the low and in many cases falling level of welfare benefits. The logical conclusion to the latter position is that governments should be spending more right away to create a larger child benefit that both increases payments for welfare families and extends this higher benefit to the working poor and other non-welfare poor families. This argument raises the issue of funding, discussed in a later section.

On the contentious issue of social assistance for children being reduced dollar for dollar of increased federal child benefits, it is not certain that welfare families would receive the full increase in federal child benefits if, instead, such families were allowed to keep the money. Over time, provinces could capture some of the federal money through stealth by delaying or foregoing increases to welfare rates or, as is increasingly the way these days, by reducing rates or making other belt-tightening changes to the welfare system such as cutting special benefits and reclassifying recipients.

Though the provinces have promised that welfare families will not be left worse off as a result of the National Child Benefit, it is difficult to imagine this voluntary condition having much meaning over time—i.e., after the provinces have reinvested their welfare savings from increased federal child benefits. Otherwise, the National Child Benefit would score a major victory in getting the provinces to agree to maintain welfare rates for families with children (more precisely, parents' benefits once children's benefits are fully removed from welfare). It would be dreaming in technicolour to hold out such a hope. But at least the provinces will not be allowed to siphon away welfare savings to purposes unrelated to child poverty.

Granted, the "reinvestment agreement" by which the provinces are supposed to reallocate welfare savings to other programs for low-income families with children cannot prevent provinces from using the extra money to offset what they would have spent anyway. B.C., for example, already financed its Family Bonus before the National Child Benefit came along; presumably, it can feel justified in using some of the increased federal benefits from the Canada Child Tax Benefit to recoup some of its costs, though welfare advocates will complain that the B.C. Family Bonus was financed partly by cuts to welfare benefits for recipients without children and the elimination of the sales tax credit for children. Nor is the reinvestment agreement likely to require provinces to index their expenditures on non-welfare programs and services for low-income families with children. However, given a sound evaluative framework, public reinvestment rules and a monitoring role for social advocates, there is probably a better chance of preventing erosion in expenditures on reinvestments than on welfare. At least the provinces have agreed to keep their welfare savings within the expenditure envelope for low-income families with children.

Interestingly, two provinces chose not to reduce welfare benefits for children by the increase in federal child benefits during the first phase of the Canada Child Tax Benefit. New Brunswick and Newfoundland passed along the federal increase to welfare families with children, presumably on the grounds that their welfare benefits for children are so low that the welfare wall is lower than in most provinces.

I would not put too much store in the long-term importance of the reinvestment process. The "reinvestment" from welfare to other programs and services for low-income families with children will be a transitional phase in the development of the National Child Benefit. It doubtless will end once Ottawa increases the Canada Child Tax Benefit to the $2,500 remove-children-from-welfare level, since at that time there will be no more provincial welfare benefits for children to displace (generally speaking—some provinces provide a few hundred dollars more on average). The $2,500 mark should be only the first objective: the federal government must keep investing in the Canada Child Tax Benefit to raise the national foundation to an adequate level (e.g., $4,000 per child) that will offset the cost of raising children for low-income families. The Canada Child Tax Benefit can be monitored and evaluated in precise terms in a way that unindexed welfare, in-kind benefits and social services cannot. In any event, in the brave new world of the Canada Health and Social Transfer, the federal government has no influence on provincial social services or welfare (apart from providing a cash incentive for provinces to remove child benefits from welfare).

In a related criticism, the reinvestment deal has been faulted for favouring the working poor, since the 1997 budget paper specified that welfare savings would go to finance programs "to assist children in low-income working families" (Department of Finance Canada 1997:19). The federal government's position is that the welfare savings it is generating by increasing federal child benefits should be reinvested in programs (income and/or services) for working poor families in order to begin lowering the welfare wall. Remember that welfare benefits for children will not end overnight, since there is a considerable distance to go before they could be fully displaced by federal child benefits.

Whether one accepts this logic or not, the fact remains that it would be difficult in practice to restrict reinvestments to programs that serve only the working poor. For example, if provinces reinvest in such provisions as school breakfast programs, child development services or child care, could and should welfare families be denied access to them? There is no longer a sharp distinction between working poor and welfare poor; some low-income families move in and out of the workforce and on and off welfare and employment insurance. Notwithstanding the welfare wall argument, the social policy and political optics of barring one group of low-income families with children from part of the National Child Benefit would be bad—and certainly would give social advocates fodder for complaint.

Interestingly, in a revamped version of the 1997 budget paper, the federal and provincial governments dropped the reference to reinvesting welfare savings in programs for "low-income working families" and spoke only of "low-income families with children" (Federal and provincial/ territorial governments 1997:11).

Another limitation of the reinvestment deal is that there is really no way for the federal government—or provincial governments, for that matter—to influence the reinvestment decisions of a particular province. The two levels of government have negotiated a framework for reinvestment that does little more than draw the boundaries of programs and services deemed acceptable for the reinvestment of welfare savings— "programs targeted at improving work incentives and supporting children in low-income families" (Department of Finance Canada 1997:16). Such programs can include income supports, earnings supplements, child support supplements, extension of in-kind benefits currently available for children in welfare families (e.g., health benefits) to working poor families, tax measures, social services (e.g., child care) and other initiatives aimed at reducing and preventing child poverty, such as child nutrition and teen parent programs (Federal and provincial/territorial governments 1997:11–12).

The range of reinvestment activities announced to date by the provinces is broad, and it seems highly unlikely that there will be any sort of standards to govern such programs. Ontario is devoting most of its initial welfare savings from the Canada Child Tax Benefit to create a provincial tax credit geared to the working poor, the Ontario Child Care Supplement for Working Families; I doubt that child care advocates will applaud such a demand-side approach that does nothing to increase the supply of child care spaces. Several other provinces are reinvesting some or all of their savings in child care, including Newfoundland, Prince Edward Island, Nova Scotia, New Brunswick, Manitoba and Alberta. Newfoundland, Prince Edward Island, Nova Scotia and Manitoba are putting welfare savings into early childhood development programs. The Northwest Territories and Saskatchewan are creating earnings supplements for working poor families with children; Québec has had such a program for years and will offer a revised version, and Alberta launched one as well. The Northwest Territories, Saskatchewan, Québec and Nova Scotia are creating income-tested child benefits along the lines of B.C.'s Family Bonus. Yukon, Alberta, Saskatchewan, Prince Edward Island and Newfoundland are extending various in-kind medical benefits for welfare recipients to all low-income children. Newfoundland is also reinvesting in youth services and Manitoba in training and job placement for the working poor (Federal and provincial/territorial governments 1998).

The claim that welfare families will get nothing from the National Child Benefit is based on the single criterion of cash benefits before and after the change. This is too narrow an evaluative approach. I think that not only the working poor, but also welfare families, will fare better under the National Child Benefit.

The Canada Child Tax Benefit and the income-tested child benefits that several provinces are providing or planning are income-tested social programs that bring none of the stigma of welfare. Instead, they are delivered anonymously and impersonally, with eligibility being determined on the basis of income as reported on the income tax return rather than assessed through the intrusive needs test used by welfare. Like the previous Child Tax Benefit, the Canada Child Tax Benefit will serve the large majority (85 percent) of Canadian families with children, including middle-income and some upper-income families. The B.C. Family Bonus is more targeted than the federal child benefit, but still serves modest-income families; benefits for a family with one or two children disappear above net family income of $33,540, which is higher than the low income cut-offs (which range in 1998 from an estimated $33,087 for a family of four living in a city of 500,000 residents or larger to $28,379 for a city of 100,000-499,999, $28,192 for a city of 30,000-99,999, $26,224 for communities under 30,000 and $22,865 for rural areas).

In an era of restraint in public spending, income-tested benefits have proven to be the safest of all income security programs in Canada. In fact, income-tested child and elderly benefits have been increased. By contrast, needs-tested welfare benefits have fallen for almost all recipients in recent years, social insurance has proven vulnerable (especially employment insurance) and universal programs—supposedly the safest of all—are extinct in the case of child and elderly benefits. Politically, the chances of improving child benefits under an income-tested National Child Benefit are far superior to winning increases in welfare benefits. In future, after the National Child Benefit has reached the $2,500 target to replace welfare benefits on behalf of children, governments can and should raise the maximum amount to improve child benefits for welfare (and other low-income) families.

An important caveat to my claim that income-tested programs have fared best is that federal child benefits—unlike elderly benefits—have been partially de-indexed since 1985. But even if federal child benefits remained partially indexed, welfare families still would be better off receiving most or all their child benefits from a partially indexed Canada Child Tax Benefit than under the current system in which the provincial portion of their child benefits (i.e., their welfare benefits for children) are unindexed. Better still, if Ottawa can be persuaded to fully index the Canada Child Tax Benefit and the provinces that offer income-tested child benefits and earnings supplements follow suit, welfare families and other low-income families will have a stable source of income from child benefits.

The welfare wall is not the only barrier to employment, but it is a real barrier nonetheless. Parents on welfare will be able to risk taking a job because they will continue receiving the Canada Child Tax Benefit and provincial child benefits in provinces that offer them; if they have to fall back on welfare, they will know that their child benefits are secure. The Canada Child Tax Benefit is analogous to the Canada Pension Plan in that it is "portable," remaining with families no matter where they work or otherwise obtain their income.

There is no question that improving work incentives is a key objective of the National Child Benefit and a major selling point to governments, particularly to those provinces that now effectively pay the full bill for welfare. The cuts to federal payments to the provinces under the Canada Health and Social Transfer will amount to about what Ottawa spent previously on provincial welfare spending, and the rising cost of caseload increases during recessions now will fall entirely on provincial treasuries. However, I doubt any National Child Benefit supporter is so naive as to believe the system's benefits (from income and services) on their own will enable large numbers of welfare recipients to leave welfare for the workforce, or will prevent families from turning to welfare if they have no other source of income.

The provinces do not need a National Child Benefit to push welfare recipients into the workforce; some provinces have reclassified welfare single parents as employable before and doubtless others will do so in future. However, a crucial issue for monitoring by advocacy groups and social policy analysts will be whether provinces cite the National Child Benefit as a rationale for reclassifying single mothers as employable or forcing them into work-for-welfare schemes. If so, then the accusation that the National Child Benefit will serve some provinces' welfare-to-work approach to welfare reform will prove to be justified.

3. The National Child Benefit is too little too late—it will have little impact on child poverty and won't abolish child poverty by 2000

There is no question that the Canada Child Tax Benefit and related provincial child benefits will not have a major impact on the rate and number of low-income children. In this sense, child benefit reform will fail to abolish child poverty by the year 2000. But apart from the fact that Parliament did not make this commitment in its 1989 resolution, the notion that an income security program like the National Child Benefit could make a major dent in the incidence of child poverty by the year 2000 is unrealistic—though perhaps not for 2010, provided Ottawa follows Caledon's advice and substantially boosts the Canada Child Tax Benefit to the $4,000 level.

In 1998, the maximum Canada Child Tax Benefit—$1,625 for one child and $1,425 for the second and each additional child, plus $213 a year for children under seven for whom child care expenses are not claimed—was not a large enough increase to significantly reduce the rate of child poverty, given the huge depth of poverty among families with children; in 1996, the average depth of poverty was $9,634 for two-parent families and $9,255 for one-parent families (Statistics Canada 1997b:37). In provinces which created income-tested child benefits of their own, total child benefits were larger, providing the province did not recoup its costs from the increase in federal child benefits.

However, the rate of poverty is not an appropriate performance indicator for the developmental stage of the National Child Benefit—setting aside the separate controversial issue of whether Statistics Canada's low income cut-offs are acceptable poverty lines, let alone standards for social programs. Because of the substantial depth of family poverty, a child benefit program that pays the same maximum amount to all low-income families with children could be judged a failure because it cannot lift many families above the poverty line (unless cost were no object). The Canadian Council on Social Development calculates that only 19 percent of low-income children lived in families within $1,500 of the poverty line in 1994, while almost half—46 percent—were in families more than $4,000 below the poverty line (CCSD 1997a:2). Yet a child benefit with a different design, one that focused its largest benefit on families *near* the poverty line, could be judged a success if its impact on the incidence of poverty were used as the standard of evaluation. The former program improves the living standards of all poor families, while the latter would help only the near-poor. Moreover, a program that moved some families just above the poverty line would leave them not much better off than before (Battle and Mendelson 1997:23–25).

Depth of poverty is a better measure of the impact of income security programs because it looks at improvements in the living standards of poor families. The federal and provincial governments were careful to specify that the National Child Benefit aims at reducing the depth of poverty. Incremental improvements in the National Child Benefit should register a decline in the total and average depth of poverty for families with children. In a study commissioned by the British Columbia government, Michael Mendelson estimated that the B.C. Family Bonus has reduced the total poverty gap for working poor families in B.C. by 19 percent, and for single-parent working poor families by 26 percent (Mendelson 1997).

As the National Child Benefit matures and if the federal government raises the maximum payment substantially, we can expect to achieve some gains in reducing the incidence as well as depth of poverty. However, even then both measures should continue to be employed. A child benefit alone cannot be expected to raise all low-income families above the poverty line; the cost would be staggering—in the order of $15 billion according to the Canadian Council on Social Development (CCSD 1997b:2). A wide range of social and employment programs is required, not just child benefits. Moreover, an increase in unemployment and/or growth in low-wage employment can swell the ranks of poor families with children and swamp increases in income programs such as child benefits, so reliance on the child poverty rate alone as the gauge of effectiveness would doom the National Child Benefit to evaluative failure. Indeed, even a depth-of-poverty measure is vulnerable to downturns in wages and increases in unemployment.

Quantitative evaluative measures alone cannot fully assess the impact of the National Child Benefit. If provinces reinvest in non-income programs, such as social services and in-kind benefits, these programs will have no direct impact on poverty as measured in income terms. Yet they doubtless will improve the living standard of families who benefit from them. Estimates of the impact of child benefits on the incidence and depth of poverty are not enough; governments and social organizations should develop additional performance indicators for the National Child Benefit and for other anti-poverty programs and policies (Battle and Mendelson 1997:28–35). It is imperative that the views of low-income families with children form a significant part of the evaluation of the National Child Benefit.

The federal government did not implement the full $850 million increase in child benefit spending in 1997, instead opting for a two-year phase-in with the Canada Child Tax Benefit coming on stream by July 1998 "or earlier if possible," though July in fact was the start date (Department of Finance Canada 1997:16). The stated reason was to allow sufficient time for negotiations with the provinces over the reinvestment agreement and to work out other administrative and data-sharing arrangements. A more cynical version is that Ottawa wanted to make sure that all provinces signed onto the National Child Benefit before the federal government upped its own ante. Subsequently, Ottawa committed a second $850 million infusion into the Canada Child Tax Benefit, though again phased in over two years (1999 and 2000).

4. The Child Tax Benefit is an inadequate down payment

- $600 million in new federal spending is a drop in the bucket compared with the billions of dollars the federal government spends on other programs, the additional billions the federal and provincial governments hand out in tax expenditures, and the $7 billion Ottawa is cutting out of federal social transfers to the provinces.
- Ottawa has the money to move much faster in investing in a substantially larger Canada Child Tax Benefit in view of its fast-disappearing deficit.

Ottawa spent $5.1 billion on the Child Tax Benefit. To boost the Canada Child Tax Benefit to the $2,500 per child level required to displace welfare benefits for children (in most provinces) will require that the federal government increase its expenditures by about $2.5 billion, bringing the total cost to about $7.5 billion.

Between the $250 million of additional spending announced in the 1996 budget and the $600 million more promised in the 1997 budget, the federal government increased its child benefits budget by $850 million, bringing federal spending to close to $6 billion in 1998—$1.5 billion short of the $7.5 billion required to reach the $2,500 per child mark to replace welfare benefits for children.

Was $850 million an adequate down payment on the National Child Benefit? In the current political climate in Ottawa, which is only now beginning to emerge from the deep freeze of expenditure restraint, $850 million was by no means a trivial amount. It represents a one-third down payment on the first-stage objective of $2.5 billion more to build the platform for an effective National Child Benefit. Moreover, during the last federal election campaign, the Liberals committed themselves to at least double the $850 million "as resources become available," (Liberal Party of Canada 1997:60) and followed through with a $850 million commitment in the 1998 budget.

Since the federal government will reach a surplus soon (through probably smaller than originally hoped), it does have the money to invest in the Canada Child Tax Benefit. Ottawa should reach the replace-welfare-benefits-for-children level of $2,500 per child by 2000, which would cost around $7.5 billion in total and just $600 million more than the $1.7

billion already committed. In 1984, when the federal child benefits system was made up of family allowances, the children's tax exemption and
the refundable child tax credit, the total cost came to $6.9 billion (in
inflation-adjusted 1998 dollars)—only $600 million short of what a $2,500
per child Canada Child Tax Benefit would cost! The extra $2.5 billion
needed to create a replace-welfare-benefits-for-children Canada Child
Tax Benefit amounts to just 2.4 percent of total federal program spending.

The $1.7 billion in "new" federal spending already committed to the
Canada Child Tax benefit may seem a paltry sum in view of the $7 billion
that Ottawa cut from its social transfer payments to the provinces under
the CHST. Even $2.5 billion in additional spending to reach the $2,500
target for the first stage would only partially recoup what the federal
government has removed from social transfers to the provinces. Of course,
the federal position is that reductions in federal social spending were
required to help put the nation's fiscal house in order. Most social groups
differ with this position, but this is all the more reason to push for
continuing increases in the Canada Child Tax Benefit and other social
programs in the coming years of federal surpluses.

5. The National Child Benefit is infected with the partial de-indexation virus

Caledon fully shares the views of other social organizations that child
benefit reform should remedy this failing of the current system. Over the
years, at the National Council of Welfare and now at Caledon, I have been
the most persistent and vociferous critic of partial de-indexation as a
mechanism of what I term "social policy by stealth" (Battle 1990). The
Tories introduced the stealth virus into federal child benefits, the personal
income tax system and the refundable GST credit; so far, the Liberals have
left intact the lucrative machinery of stealth.

Partial de-indexation has gradually eroded the value of federal child
benefits and offset increases that the Conservatives made to the refundable child tax credit in the mid-1980s. The same thing will happen to the
Canada Child Tax Benefit if it remains partially indexed; a portion of its
gains will be lost to inflation each year. The "inflation over 3 percent"
formula that has been in operation for over a decade means that the value
of child benefits declines by three percent a year if inflation is over three
percent, or by the amount of inflation if the cost of living increases by less
than three percent. Moreover, partial de-indexation also steadily lowers
the real level of the net family income threshold for maximum benefits.
Maximum payments are targeted further and further down the income
ladder over the years, fewer low-income families receive the maximum
amount and the "disappearing point"—the income level where eligibility
for benefits ends—also falls with each passing year, gradually moving

from upper-middle-income to middle-income families. Every family loses from partial de-indexation, but its impact is regressive; the decline in benefits hits families with low incomes hardest in relative terms.

It is essential that the federal government fully index the Canada Child Tax Benefit. However, that progressive change would increase Ottawa's costs, since partial de-indexation is estimated to save $170 million a year (CCSD 1997b:3). Moreover, the federal government will be reluctant to give up the fiscal advantages of a stealthy automatic-cuts mechanism, which brings little if any political pain since no one outside of a handful of social policy experts and advocates understands what is going on.

Provincial welfare benefits, including those paid on behalf of children, are not indexed at all. Provincial governments reap even larger fiscal rewards from this policy of stealth than they would if they followed the federal practice of at least partially indexing benefits. Simply by freezing parents' welfare rates, provincial governments can claim to be honouring their commitment not to leave welfare families with children worse off after child benefit reform, while in reality steadily reducing the value of welfare incomes. I doubt that provinces can be persuaded to index their welfare rates or their income-tested child benefits. However, social advocates still should make that case on the basis of the supposed commitment of the provinces not to leave welfare families worse off as a result of the National Child Benefit.

This point raises another argument in favour of the National Child Benefit. To the extent that welfare families will receive more of their child benefits from the federal government—and eventually most, if not all— then they will be better off because Ottawa at least partially indexes its child benefits. If social groups can convince the federal government to fully index the Canada Child Tax Benefit, then welfare families will be even better off than they are at present.

6. The National Child Benefit will result in an even more polyglot child benefits system with no national standards

The "reinvestment agreement" is a sort of back door, softly-softly form of conditional cost-sharing. The provinces agree to spend their federally enabled savings on welfare benefits for children on other programs for low-income families with children. As noted earlier, however, I think the reinvestment deal will give the provinces wide latitude about where and how to spend their savings from federally displaced welfare benefits for children. It is hard to imagine the provinces, flush with their freedom of action in the new laissez-faire era of the Canada Health and Social Transfer, agreeing to any process that tried to develop and apply conditions or standards to their various programs and services for low-income families with children. Moreover, the reinvestment deal likely will be time-limited, fading away once the federal government has raised the Canada Child Tax Benefit to a level considered sufficient to displace welfare benefits for children.

The real hope for national standards in child benefits lies with the federal government. Over time, Ottawa will assume a growing share of the income component of the National Child Benefit and should raise that level even higher than the replace-welfare-benefits-for-children mark to cover the cost of raising a child for low-income families. There is no better way to ensure national standards than through a federal income security program. Granted, Québec has always invested more than other provinces in family policy and is unlikely to give up its new integrated family allowance program if Ottawa raises its national platform over the years. (B.C., Saskatchewan, New Brunswick and any other provinces that go the provincial child benefit route also will have to decide how to adjust their benefits to a rising federal child benefit foundation.) But the benign result would be a higher combined federal-Québec level of child benefits for Québec's low-income families.

The federal Working Income Supplement has not worked. Experience will show if the provinces are better able to design and deliver earnings supplements. Québec already provides such a program, though the take-up apparently is low; B.C., Alberta, Saskatchewan and New Brunswick are introducing versions of their own. Provinces can design earnings supplements that mesh with their minimum wages and welfare systems and that take into account the number and distribution of low-earning families. Conceivably, they also can make use of the existing welfare administrative machinery to help adjust for fluctuating family incomes that cannot easily be handled by the federal Canada Child Tax Benefit which relies upon the annual income tax return for assessing family income.

Provincial wage supplements as well as in-kind benefits and social services considered to be part of the National Child Benefit System doubtless will continue to be diverse and not subject to any kind of enforceable national standards. Whether the National Child Benefit will increase, leave the same or decrease the variability of provincial child benefits (cash and services) is a question for future empirical study. Perhaps provinces will look closely at and learn from each others' experiences, though that sharing of knowledge will not necessarily lead to less variation in the nature and quality of their various programs. But I doubt that the National Child Benefit will lead to any more variability in provincial programs than already exists under the Canada Health and Social Transfer. However, to the extent that it increases the federal role in (cash) child benefits, the National Child Benefit will improve existing national standards in income support for low-income families with children.

7. Canada needs a comprehensive plan with a wide range of social and economic measures—a national child poverty project—not just a National Child Benefit

I could not agree more, and along with social advocates, I have made this case repeatedly over the years. Governments are now working on a National Children's Agenda.

However, the National Child Benefit should be judged on its own merits, not faulted for failing to be part of a comprehensive, multi-faceted and concerted strategy against child poverty. If governments claim that the National Child Benefit is a sufficient response to child poverty—and they would be foolish to do so—then it is governments, not child benefits, that should take the heat.

Conclusion

Social groups have every reason to be sceptical about any social policy initiative in this era of reduction by "reform." However, they should not be so quick to throw the baby bonus out with the bathwater. The test will be how the venture develops over the coming years. Social groups must be vigilant and conduct their own assessments of the development of the National Child Benefit to provide Canadians with a critical counterpoint to government evaluations.

The launch of the Canada Child Tax Benefit and associated provincial reinvestment in programs for low-income families with children is just that: a launch. The dream of an integrated child benefit cannot be achieved until the provinces no longer deliver income benefits for children through their welfare systems.

The federal government can and should boost child benefits to deliver the $2,500 per child required to displace welfare benefits for children by the year 2000. But that is only the first objective. By 2010 at the latest, Ottawa should reach the second major target of a $4,000 per child benefit that would cover (by conservative estimate) the cost of raising a child for low-income families. Then the federal government will have created for all poor children what it has already achieved for all poor seniors—a *de facto* guaranteed income that will significantly reduce the risk and depth of poverty. Such a National Child Benefit would provide the necessary platform on which to mount effective social services, employment programs, community supports and the many other weapons needed to wage a real war on family poverty.

3

Income Security and the Labour Market:
Saskatchewan Perspectives on Child Benefit Reform

Rick August

Recent decades have seen major changes in our economy, labour market and social relationships, which have increased demand for income security programs. Until now we have allowed most of this increased demand to devolve upon welfare-type programs. As a result, welfare has expanded from having a relatively small role in the 1960s to being a system that now touches the lives of a significant portion of the population. In setting the scene for child benefit reform in Saskatchewan, this chapter will argue that the social assistance or welfare model of income support is inadequate for this expanded role.

Welfare is structured to ensure that, in the absence of other resources, citizens' basic needs will be met. Generally speaking, welfare is effective at preventing destitution, but it does so at considerable public expense, administrative effort and intrusion into citizens' private lives. Welfare also draws its beneficiaries into a paternalistic relationship with the state, which isolates them from the economic and social mainstream and often forces them to sacrifice long-term interests to satisfy immediate needs.

Saskatchewan is pursuing strategic directions for income security reform which are based on alternatives to the social assistance model. These alternatives are intended to meet community standards of social justice and fairness, but also maintain their program constituents as much as possible within the mainstream of human activity. Child benefit reform in Saskatchewan is part of this strategic direction.

Child benefit reform will strengthen direct transfers to poor families, but its main focus is on encouraging low-income parents to work. This is a recognition of reality, not a moral judgement. Public benefits notwithstanding, in a market economy work is the principle means of distributing income and the most likely route out of poverty. Current income security programs often penalize people who work. Child benefit reform will not guarantee that there will be sufficient good jobs available for low-income parents, but it can ensure that working is a rational economic choice.

Child benefit reform is primarily a strategy to manage the relationship between wages and benefits. Friction between work and welfare is rarely significant for persons without dependents, but families with children have additional needs which market wages do not recognize. In many cases, the best possible expectation of income from market wages can be less than the income needed to provide a family with the basic necessities of life.

When only social assistance is available to bridge this gap, low-income parents will be drawn to welfare to meet their needs. Once in the welfare system, families face significant barriers and disincentives to work. The family is supported at a minimum living standard by public transfer payments, but are still poor and living within an incentive structure that effectively encourages them to remain so. Child benefit reform is an attempt to change this incentive structure, helping low-income parents to increase market incomes and raise their families' living standards.

Saskatchewan has implemented a number of measures aimed at improving work incentives for low-income parents. The core of the reform, however, is the separation of children's benefits from the welfare system. If support for children's needs can be made available through an alternate structure which allows low-income working families to retain their child benefits, the presence of children will be less of a factor in pushing families into the welfare trap, and parents will be better able to compete with singles and childless couples for available work.

Other methods have been tried in the past to reduce the friction between income security and the labour market. In Saskatchewan in the 1980s, for example, benefits were restricted and reduced to try to make work more attractive relative to welfare. This strategy produced short-term reductions in social assistance caseloads, but these reductions were not sustained over time. The benefit reduction strategy may also have forced families deeper into financial distress, contributing to high levels of child and family poverty in the years that followed.

It is important that changes to child benefits be viewed in context. The issue of child poverty is a complicated one, and most observers agree that a solution will require not only income-related measures but action on a wide range of program and policy fronts. Child benefits should not be viewed as a quick fix, but rather as one piece of a larger anti-poverty strategy.

The changes underway in Saskatchewan are taking place within a national context of social program renewal, in particular the National Child Benefit initiative. The National Child Benefit is a co-operative arrangement among governments which has great potential to improve programs for children and low-income families. It could also signal the beginning of a basic change of direction for Canada's income security system, away from reliance on individualized, stigmatizing welfare programs and towards greater reliance on policies that address income needs in a broader social and economic context. If this proves to be the case, the National Child Benefit may help us achieve an income security system for Canada that is more effective, more respectful of individual dignity, better integrated into the economy at large and more acceptable to the general public than our current approaches.

The Labour Market and the Structure
of Income Security Programs

Market Forces

Figure 1 shows results from an analysis of Saskatchewan market income trends carried out by the Canadian Council on Social Development. This analysis may provide some insight into the much-discussed issue of labour market restructuring and its effect on the poor.

The analysis focuses on the change in market income, adjusted for

Figure 1

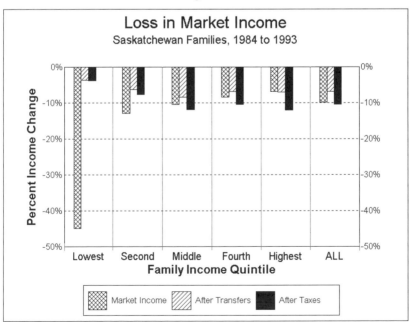

(Source: See Notes to Figures)

inflation, among Saskatchewan wage-earner families with children in the reference years 1984 and 1993.[1]

These data indicate that families with children at all income levels experienced an average loss of market income of $4,568 in 1993 dollars, or 9.8 percent, before taking into account the effect of taxes and income transfers by governments. Government transfer payments reduced the average market income loss to 6.8 percent, while the tax burden increased the net income loss to a relatively modest 10.4 percent.

The situation is much more dramatic, however, if one focuses on the lowest income group among families. For the lowest quintile, the CCSD analysis shows a slightly lower dollar decline in market income of $3,136. In proportional terms, however, this represents a full 44.9 percent decline in market income between the reference years. After transfer payments from government and a minor income-tax effect the net loss is reduced to 3.7 percent.

The role of transfers in shielding families from labour market effects is striking, and somewhat reassuring. However, all forms of transfer payment are not alike in their impact on family circumstance. Federal children's benefits and child-related tax measures, which had a relatively

Figure 2

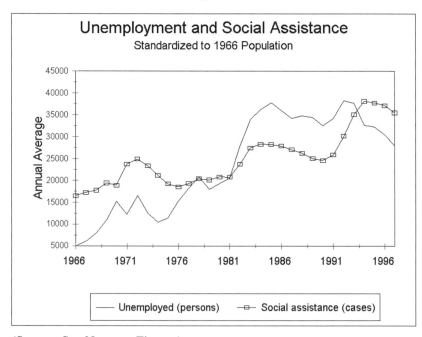

(Source: See Notes to Figures)

stable form throughout the reference period of these data, no doubt had a significant role in buffering income losses. However, evidence from social assistance caseload trends also suggest welfare played an increasingly important part in replacing families' lost market income.

Both unemployment and social assistance have been on a long-term upward trend in Saskatchewan, as in Canada as a whole. As Figure 2 shows, both indicators have risen sharply in recessionary periods, but have not recovered fully in economic upswings. The result is a ratcheting-up effect over time of baseline unemployment and social assistance dependency. Overall caseloads for social assistance, which were about 20,000 thirty years ago, were roughly double that number at the peak of the last recession in the early 1990s. On a population-adjusted basis, the number of families with children on social assistance in Saskatchewan increased by over 23 percent between 1984 and 1993, the reference years for the CCSD analysis.

Work and Welfare

There is cause for concern in having such a large number of young, working-age families forced to rely on welfare. Social assistance was not designed to act as a primary income support program for people with strong labour force attachment. To qualify for welfare, families must be very poor and must have depleted most of the assets and other resources that can help carry an economically marginal family through temporary hard times. An economic descent to welfare eligibility levels often means a family can expect a longer spell of poverty, and a harder fight to get back into the economic mainstream.

Depletion of assets is not the only problem. Because welfare was designed to ensure that basic needs are met, the amount of benefits increases with the number of people in a family unit. Wage rates, on the other hand, depend primarily on market forces. Regulated minimum wage rates were historically oriented towards the single earner, and it is very rare for wages to vary according to the employee's family needs. In short, welfare is responsive to family needs, while wages are not. Figure 3 illustrates some aspects of this point, using pre-reform benefit structures in Saskatchewan as an example. The approximate gross earnings level for an individual working full time at Saskatchewan minimum wage is used as a notional reference point for comparison with government benefits. One can see that the benefits available to an individual are significantly lower than this earnings reference point. A single person working roughly half-time at minimum wage would already be out of the social assistance structure.

Where basic needs are low, as in the case of single persons, or where wages are high, this discontinuity is not a major issue. However, in cases

Figure 3

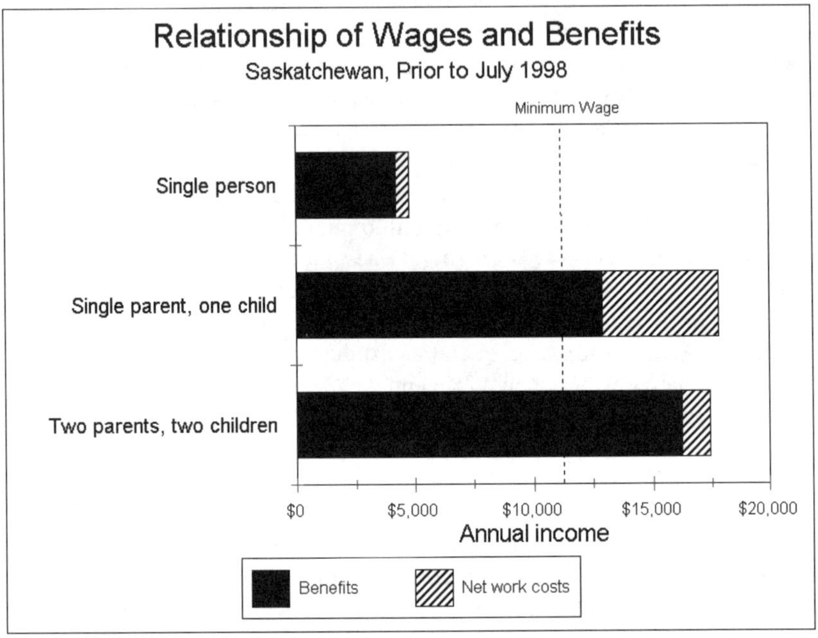

Relationship of Wages and Benefits
Saskatchewan, Prior to July 1998

(Source: See Notes to Figures)

where adults with dependent children, who have relatively high needs, only have access to low-wage work, the weakness of welfare as an income support structure begins to become more evident.

The comparison between the wage reference and benefits is quite different, however, for families with children. In these cases benefits are higher than the earnings from a minimum wage job. When the added costs of going out to work are considered—many of them explicitly child-related like day care—a parent's net earnings potential can compare even less favourably with benefits, especially for single parents who lack the additional resources brought to the family by a second adult.

The different wage-to-benefit relationship for singles compared with families is important from the point of view of developing strategies to help people get into the workforce. For singles, the short-term goal of escaping social assistance is arguably within reach when work is available. For a person with dependents, however, even if full-time work is available, the family may still be on welfare and may still be living well below generally accepted poverty standards.

Work and welfare are not a comfortable fit. As a program of last resort, social assistance operates on the "budget deficit" system. Benefit rates are set to represent the minimum amount necessary to cover basic needs. To determine actual benefits, an applicant's resources are measured against needs, and the difference paid as benefit. This means that most types of income—child maintenance, Canada Pension disability benefits, etc.—result in a dollar-for-dollar benefit reduction.

In the case of employment income, modest earnings exemptions are allowed so that the beneficiary has some incentive to work. However, even with earnings exemptions, a recipient still faces a high rate of benefit reduction relative to earnings. In Saskatchewan's pre-reform programs, welfare benefits were reduced by 80 percent to 100 percent of earnings at most income ranges. These welfare tax-back rates can sometimes overlap with income tax and other programs' benefit reduction rates, producing net tax rates of over 100 percent. In these situations, working is, quite literally, a money-losing proposition.[2]

Those on social assistance who have an opportunity to take a job can face other barriers in addition to high tax-back rates. When a social assistance recipient takes a job, welfare will attempt to support this work effort by providing benefits for child care, transportation and other work expenses. This has the effect of raising overall benefits, and thus raising the income threshold to escape welfare's high tax-back rates. It also sets up a considerable disincentive to step over the eligibility threshold, because these costs will then fall upon the individual, eroding the disposable income value of earnings.

Health coverage can also be an issue. In Saskatchewan, as in other provinces, public health care does not cover all possible costs. Because social assistance recipients do not have the resources to buy health services, they are provided with much more comprehensive health coverage than the general public. The end of cash benefit entitlement also usually means the end of this supplementary health coverage. Reduced health care coverage pushes the cost of working one's way off of social assistance even higher.

These factors and others comprise a cluster of barriers and disincentives which can make it quite difficult for welfare families to improve their circumstances. Taking advantage of a work opportunity could result in less income, fewer services and lower living standards for both the parent and children. The combined effect of these factors, which some refer to as the "welfare wall," can be seen in the workforce involvement, or lack thereof, of welfare parents. In the period just prior to benefit restructuring in July 1998, only about 17 percent of Saskatchewan social assistance families with children reported any employment earnings.

One frequently hears suggestions that welfare recipients would work if the jobs were there for them. All else being equal, this would no doubt be the case, for evidence suggests that most people prefer to be active, productive and disentangled from programs like social assistance. And as has been argued above, deteriorating labour market conditions are surely a factor in creating higher welfare dependency, particularly among families. However, more and better jobs may simply not be enough to solve the family poverty problem. With welfare acting in an income supplementation role, parents may simply be unable to afford to take advantage of job opportunities.

Structural reform of children's benefits is an attempt to provide income security for children without hindering parents' attachment to the labour market. The premise behind child benefit reform is not that jobs will appear for welfare parents because they have stronger incentives. The goal is to reduce the relative competitive disadvantage in the labour market of parents compared with those without dependents.

If this goal is accomplished, parents' work efforts should be more successful even in a fixed labour market. Obviously, the scope of success of this strategy will be affected by the quality and availability of jobs. Without structural reform, however, low-income families with children may remain poor and economically isolated, even in an improved job market, because "the system" makes working an unattractive or nonviable choice for individual poor families.

Previous Reform Efforts

The approach of Saskatchewan child benefit reform (and the National Child Benefit) is to reduce the inequity between working and non-working families by increasing working parents' access to benefits for children. This is far from a new idea. In fact, the national social assistance reforms of the mid-1960s were barely complete when work began towards closing a known gap in the social security system, the lack of support for the working poor. In the early 1970s a federal–provincial study team proposed a national income supplementation program for low-income families, which would, it was argued, help maintain low-income working families living outside the welfare system.

The fiscal position of governments and the climate for social program reform changed rapidly in the mid-1970s, however, and the national program failed to materialize as planned, although the federal government did introduce its own modest benefit for working poor families in 1978.[3] Through most of the last three decades, however, the main income support vehicle for low-income families has continued to be welfare, with all its negative as well as positive impacts.

Saskatchewan was one of a very few jurisdictions that decided to try to move ahead in the 1970s, in anticipation of a national income supplementation program, with reform of programs for the working poor. The

Family Income Plan (FIP), introduced in 1974, was an income-tested program[4] which made child benefits available at a rate equivalent to children's welfare to low-income families, whether parents were working or not, and whether the family was on welfare or not.

In its early days, FIP was a popular alternative to social assistance for the working poor. Unfortunately, when hopes for a national program framework collapsed, the FIP experiment lost its momentum. Parallel child benefits were still available from welfare, and in a high-inflation period, fiscal decisions were made over time, which priorized social assistance over FIP. The program gradually lost its caseload and its effectiveness as its benefits fell behind those available from welfare for children. Families who had formerly used FIP to supplement earnings drifted back to social assistance. As Figure 4 shows, FIP caseloads dwindled over time to a relative handful of families.

Figure 4

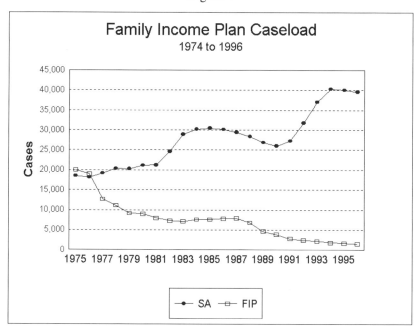

(Source: See Notes to Figures)

Child Poverty

The problem that motivated Saskatchewan to create FIP did not go away, however. In fact, from the early 1980s on, evidence suggests that a larger proportion of families gathered in the statuses of the working poor and welfare poor. Figure 5 shows the incidence of children living in low-income families in Saskatchewan since 1980.[5] For comparison purposes, the same statistic for senior citizens is also shown on the chart. The contrast between the income trends of the two groups is clear. Seniors now benefit from a solid social security system, largely built up since the 1960s, which was aimed explicitly at improving living standards among the elderly. Seniors are also much more isolated from changes in labour market conditions. Compared with 1980, relatively few Saskatchewan seniors have incomes lower than the low income cut-off (LICO) standard, and very few are poor enough to qualify under much lower welfare standards.[6]

By comparison, children in low-income families have fared poorly. Labour market restructuring, a significant increase in the number of vulnerable single parent families,[7] and lack of progress in resolving the friction between work and benefits are all factors which no doubt have contributed to this trend.

Figure 5

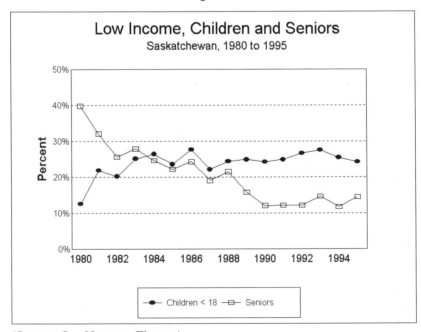

(Source: See Notes to Figures)

National Child Benefit

In the early 1990s a great deal of work was being undertaken in government to develop options for child benefit reform. Ontario officials had developed detailed plans for an income-tested provincial child benefit plan before shelving the project for fiscal reasons. Saskatchewan had been working since 1992 on proposals for reform, but also had to hold back for fiscal reasons. An integrated federal–provincial benefit program for children was included as an option in the 1994 federal social security review, along with several options for unilateral federal reform, but federal budget reductions in 1995 put the issue of national child benefit reform on hold again. Most governments at that time had not yet re-established the fiscal capacity for major new social programs. Only British Columbia, to its credit, proceeded on its own resources to launch an income-tested child benefit, the Family Bonus, in 1996.

When set to the task of "social policy renewal" in the wake of federal cuts, governments were quick to revive the notion of an integrated national benefit program for children. The idea would gain a surprising degree of momentum, including endorsement by Canada's first ministers in 1996. A working group of officials from governments across Canada was formed to negotiate the concrete details of such a program, which ultimately resulted in the launch of the first stages of the National Child Benefit (NCB) initiative in July 1998.

The National Child Benefit is an agreement entered into by federal, provincial and territorial governments to restructure programs at both levels of government aimed at low-income families.[8] The initiative has three goals—to reduce child poverty, to support labour force attachment for low-income families and to increase the harmonization and efficiency of the overall income security system for families.

Under the NCB initiative, the federal government will assume greater responsibility for income support for children. Beginning in July 1998, a new tier of benefits for low-income families, the National Child Benefit Supplement, was added to the former Child Tax Benefit system, and the combined new structure was renamed the Canada Child Tax Benefit.

This new benefit tier is intended to displace provincial and territorial children's benefits paid through social assistance. The NCB supplement is expected to increase over time until it replaces basic welfare benefits for children in all parts of the country.[9] At the point that the NCB supplement has replaced children's welfare, children's income support and child poverty will primarily be a matter of national social policy, addressed through a national social program.

The federal increases to children's income support will create savings as they displace provincial welfare. Participant governments have agreed that at least the amount of these savings be "reinvested" in some form of benefits, programs and services for low-income families which are consistent with the three basic NCB goals.

Shifting children's benefits to the national income-tested platform is more costly for governments than welfare, but produces several major advantages. The federal benefit is broad-based, reaching 80 percent of all families in Canada. Paying child benefits to low-income families through this system does not isolate low-income families from the middle class to the same degree that welfare does. Families are required to apply for benefits only once, when they have a new child in the family, and monthly benefits are based on family income information from the tax system.

This system is efficient, relatively non-intrusive, and distinct from the welfare administrative style, in that income is the sole determinant of benefits for a given family size. These factors will be important for the long-term acceptance of the program by beneficiaries and the general public. Those receiving federal child benefits do not think of themselves as "dependent" in the sense that they might if the benefit came from welfare.

Most importantly, the federal benefit system allows child benefits to reach families with significantly higher earning levels than does social assistance. It is expected that this factor should increase employment income, since parents will know that as they earn more money their children's benefits will be withdrawn only gradually, until they reach a somewhat more comfortable living standard.

The other major outcome of the National Child Benefit will be an expansion of programs and services for lower-income families at the provincial and territorial level. The range of reinvestment programs and services for the first stage of the NCB included work income supplements, child care enrichments, extended health benefits, and several other types of new benefits. Many jurisdictions, including Saskatchewan, invested more in the first stage of the NCB than they were required to under NCB reinvestment parameters. The reinvestment pool will be refreshed in stages as the NCB matures, up to the point where provincial/territorial social assistance is completely subsumed by the NCB supplement.

The National Child Benefit is the first major national social policy initiative in over thirty years. It is also the first to place a strong emphasis on multilateral co-operation and consensus, open reporting to the public and accountability for program outcomes, rather than just outputs. Some believe that the NCB process will become a model for intergovernmental relations and future social program development in Canada.

Saskatchewan Child Benefit Reform

The benefit changes that were implemented in July 1998 in Saskatchewan are part of a wider process of restructuring of income security and related programs. The goal of reform is to reorient benefit and service programs so that they support independence and self-sufficiency. For income support programs, this means less reliance on passive transfers and more emphasis on encouraging activities which are productive for the individual and the province as a whole.

The core strategy of Saskatchewan income security reform is to develop program and policy instruments that act as substitutes for aspects of the welfare system. New program elements should provide at least the same degree of income security protection as welfare, but should also consistently encourage clients to act in their own best interests.[10]

Child benefit restructuring means more than just realignment of transfer payments. The province is attempting to move towards a client–program relationship that more closely resembles the type of relationship that citizens in the economic mainstream form in the course of their daily lives. For this reason, the administrative changes that accompany benefit restructuring are as important as the changes to the alignment of benefits.

Saskatchewan Child Benefit

The centrepiece of Saskatchewan child benefit reform, at least in its early stages, is the Saskatchewan Child Benefit (SCB). This program began making payments in July 1998. The structural role of the SCB is to simulate, as far as Saskatchewan's finances allow, the same relationship between income security and the labour market that low-income families would experience under a relatively mature form of the National Child Benefit.

Had Saskatchewan chosen not to implement the SCB and continued to provide residual support for children through social assistance, the province's reaction to higher federal child benefits from the NCB supplement would have been either to reduce rates for children across the board or to account for the federal increase in each family's welfare budget. Benefits to low-income working families would have accrued gradually as the federal benefit increased.

Because child poverty is a high priority issue, Saskatchewan chose an approach that is intended to bring these benefits into place more quickly. The SCB converts the remainder of provincial welfare for children to an income-tested benefit, with a much broader base than welfare. Benefit levels were set so that the combined total maximum benefit of the new NCB supplement and the SCB is equal to the former basic social assistance benefit for children.[11] This ensures that welfare families have the same level of support that they formerly had available from social assistance.

The SCB, however, is available to families with higher incomes than is welfare. Under the old structure most families had exhausted welfare benefits by the time they reached $12–15,000 in earnings. Under the SCB families are eligible for benefits up to approximately $26,000, or higher in the case of larger families.[12] For this reason it reaches many low-income working families who did not qualify under the old system. The total number of children for whom benefits were paid under the old structure in June 1998 by either provincial or federal (on-reserve) welfare was approximately 46,000. In August 1998, with the new program in place, benefits from the SCB and its federal parallel were paid for over 92,000 children.[13]

This broader support for low-income families should begin to relieve the economic pressures on working families which can push them into social assistance, and will lower some of the barriers to working for those already in the welfare system.

As in the case of the NCB Supplement, the SCB is more expensive than social assistance because its reach is broader. This investment of public funds is expected to pay off over time, however, as more families leave social assistance for work, and fewer working families are forced onto welfare. Moreover, working poor families will have the benefit of more direct support from government and hopefully more market income from employment.

The Saskatchewan Child Benefit is a program with a limited lifespan, because it is expected to be subsumed over time by increases to the National Child Benefit Supplement. To avoid building a separate delivery administration and to keep programs as simple as possible for clients, the province negotiated an arrangement with Revenue Canada to integrate the provincial SCB benefit with federal child benefit payments.

The integrated option allows the province, like the federal government, to determine benefits using information families have already supplied with their annual income tax returns. As long as families have applied for the CCTB and filed their tax returns, the SCB is automatically delivered monthly.[14]

Saskatchewan Employment Supplement

The new Saskatchewan Employment Supplement (SES), which also began in July 1998, is a further element of Saskatchewan's income security program redesign. The main purpose of the SES is to act as an employment support for low-income parents, offsetting some of the work costs parents accrue because of their children.

The program is structured differently from traditional income security programs, which generally pay families less as their income rises.

Over certain income ranges, SES pays families more benefits as their earnings increase. This is based on the presumption that for parents in low-wage jobs, higher earnings mean more hours worked, and thus greater child-related work costs. Benefit rates are subject to a maximum, and are reduced by income above a certain threshold to ensure the program is targeted to only low-income families.[15]

The SES program could in some ways be seen as a successor to the federal Working Income Supplement (WIS) which ended in June 1998 with the launch of the NCB and had a similar benefit structure in some respects. Although the WIS was administered from the tax system and therefore was paid automatically to families who qualified, there was a long lag—six to eighteen months—between earnings and benefits. This delay was believed to undermine its effectiveness at offsetting parents' work expenses.

SES, on the other hand, requires a family to make an application for benefits and report income at least quarterly, but the supplement is received with much less delay than the WIS. Families reporting earnings for a benefit month will receive SES the following month. The benefits are generally higher, at least at lower income ranges, and more responsive to family size than the federal program.[16] In theory at least, SES should be more effective at neutralizing child-related work costs for low-income parents.

Application-driven programs like the SES, however, have the disadvantage of requiring a declarative act by each family wanting to receive benefits. People are surprisingly resistant to applying for government programs, and compared with "automatic" benefits like the WIS, SES could be expected to have more difficulty reaching its target group. SES needs to attract working poor families outside the current welfare system to achieve its policy goals.

In the design of an administrative model for SES, Saskatchewan attempted to address potential take-up problems, as well as to create a different style of program–client interaction. The SES administration is quite different from Saskatchewan's more traditional income security programs. Application and income reporting is by telephone only, and the application/reporting process is nearly "paper free." Beneficiaries report income changes as they occur, or at least once per quarter, either to an extended-hour telephone client service centre or through an automated telephone reporting system. Benefit payments are made by electronic funds transfer to clients' bank accounts.

Although SES is aimed primarily at the working poor, it is also available to welfare families. Social assistance earnings exemption policies have been modified to co-ordinate with SES, and to ensure that overall rewards from work are greater for welfare families than they were before program restructuring.[17] Figure 6 show the approximate structure of federal and provincial child benefits in their July 1998 form for a two-parent family with two children. Figure 7 shows the net effect of the change, after federal and provincial income taxes are considered. The new structure protects the current level of benefit entitlement at very low incomes, while providing a greater net benefit as income rises towards the working poor range. The greatest impact is on families in the $15–25,000 income range. Families in this category currently receive less support from government than do welfare families.

Maintenance income

The incidence of poverty among single parent families is very high. The recent National Longitudinal Survey of Children and Youth noted that over 70 percent of children of single parents in 1994 lived in families with incomes below the LICO standard. Judging from welfare utilization, many seem to have incomes well below the LICO standards. In Saskatchewan about one-third of single parents are on social assistance in any given month, and up to half will need welfare benefits over the course of a year.[18]

While poverty among single parents is obviously a complex issue, more support to children from non-custodial parents could help a significant number of single-parent families. While a number of mechanisms are

Figure 6

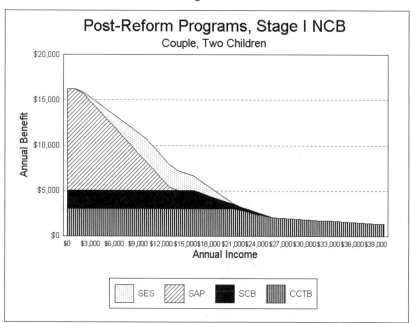

(Source: See Notes to Figures)

already in place to support enforcement of maintenance agreements, the results remain inconsistent. Although it is technically mandatory, for example, for single parents on social assistance to pursue maintenance income, less than 25 percent of single parents on welfare actually report maintenance income. While there could be a number of explanations for low maintenance income among welfare single parents, it is likely that incentives—or lack of incentives—play a role. Establishing and enforcing maintenance agreements or orders can often be difficult, but for a family on social assistance, receiving maintenance has not improved family circumstances because maintenance is deducted dollar-for-dollar from entitlement.

Saskatchewan is attempting to address this situation by treating maintenance income as if it was employment income for purposes of SES. This allows some benefit from maintenance payments to flow through to welfare families, and also increases the positive impact of maintenance payments on families above the welfare threshold. It is an experimental policy, and one that will be watched with interest in the evaluative process. Hopefully, inclusion of maintenance within the definition of supplementable income will support overall efforts to reduce poverty among single parent families.

Figure 7

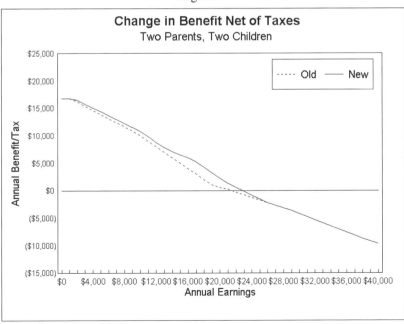

(Source: See Notes to Figures)

Family Health Benefits

Saskatchewan's system of universal public health insurance covers many but not all health costs. Social assistance recipients receive supplementary health coverage which allows them to obtain most medical and dental services either free or at much reduced cost.[19] To ensure that loss of these supplementary health benefits is not a deterrent to leaving welfare, Saskatchewan has changed the basis for entitlement from a welfare-based eligibility key to a system based on family income. All families qualifying for income-tested provincial child benefits from the SCB or the SES will qualify for the new Family Health Benefits program. Children in eligible families will receive the same coverage as social assistance families. The new program also includes a more limited package of supplementary health benefits for adults.[20]

Saskatchewan Assistance Plan

The first stage of child benefit reform resulted in a number of changes to the Saskatchewan Assistance Plan (SAP), the province's social assistance program. The most important change is the removal of allowances for basic food, clothing and personal needs of children from the SAP benefit schedule. After July 1998, the income-tested federal–provincial benefit structure is the main source of support for children's basic needs.

Figure 8 shows the effect of implementation of the new child benefit programs on thresholds for families to leave social assistance. Removing basic children's allowances from welfare reduces the welfare threshold for families by roughly $1,500 per child per year. The new flat-rate earnings exemption for SAP families also reduces welfare thresholds. Given that all the benefits removed from welfare have been replaced from non-welfare sources, this narrowing of the scope of welfare is a positive outcome of reform. Many families with relatively marginal welfare entitlements in the old system will no longer need social assistance benefits. Lower thresholds should also encourage more parents to work, since the level of incremental earnings needed to leave welfare is lower once children's benefits and part of the earnings exemption are removed.

The first stage of child benefit reform achieves the notional goal of taking children out of welfare, at least with respect to basic income support. For the foreseeable future, however, a number of welfare features related to children will remain in social assistance. Welfare shelter rates will still recognize the presence of children in the family. Social assistance is also better equipped to respond to irregular needs such as school supplies and any other special needs of children. Nonetheless, the 1998 changes implemented move the Saskatchewan Assistance Plan a significant step closer to an "adults only" program.

Next Steps

Child benefit reform is a structural approach to child poverty. As such, it will be important not to look for instant results, nor to assess the outcome of program changes in isolation. Structural reform should improve the competitive position of low-income parents so that regardless of the state of the economy, poor families with children begin to do better in relative terms. Still, a large measure of the absolute success or failure of child benefit reform will depend on developments in the economy, the labour market, in tax and fiscal policies and in other externalities.

Reforms aimed at family economics and the labour market are also only one piece of a much larger puzzle. Hopefully, the high public profile of the National Child Benefit will help focus attention on the many other issues which need to be addressed in a comprehensive child poverty strategy. At a provincial level, the NCB and child benefit reform form part of a broader planning initiative, Saskatchewan's Action Plan for Children. The National Children's Agenda, now being discussed by federal, provincial and territorial officials, could serve a similar integrative function on a national level.

The emergence of consensus around a National Child Benefit is a sign

Figure 8

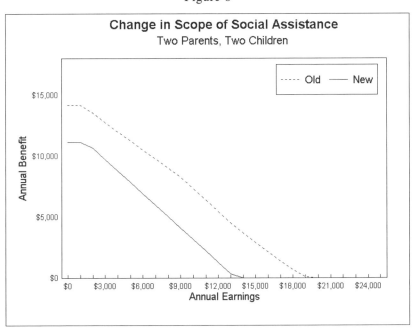

(Source: See Notes to Figures)

that the well-being of children has moved forward as a national social policy priority. The changes to federal child benefits and the enrichment of provincial and territorial programs within the context of the National Child Benefit will not ensure a victory in the fight against child poverty, but these changes are an important start, and a concrete signal of governments' renewed commitment to progress against child poverty.

Notes to Figures

Figure 1: Data are from an unpublished analysis by the Canadian Council on Social Development using Statistics Canada microdata files from the Survey of Consumer Finance. Incomes are in constant 1993 dollars. The data pertain to an estimated population of 85,752 Saskatchewan families with at least one child under the age of eighteen living at home, and without self-employment income (positive or negative) in either 1984 or 1993. All inferences drawn from the CCSD data are the responsibility of this writer.

Figure 2: The population series used to standardize caseload and unemployment values is from the Saskatchewan Bureau of Statistics. Numbers of unemployed persons are from Statistics Canada publication 71-201-XPB. The historical social assistance caseload series is derived from Saskatchewan Social Services internal reports. For a parallel discussion of national trends, readers might wish to refer to a 1994 publication by Human Resources Development Canada (HDRC 1994), *Social Security in Canada* (catalogue number CS-001-1-94), a background document produced in connection with the recent social security review.

Figure 3: Program structures are as of June 1998. Benefits are based on actual average Saskatchewan social assistance needs in October 1997 plus Goods and Services Tax Rebate and Child Tax Benefit. Gross annual minimum wage earnings are assumed as 2,000 hours at $5.60 per hour, or $11,200 per year. Work costs include $540 per year per family unit for transportation. This is a common amount for a welfare travel allowance. Also included is child care: for the single parent with one child 2000 hours at $2.50 per hour; for the couple with two children 500 hours at $3.35 per hour. These costs are based on rates in the Provincial Training Allowance program. Work costs are discounted by the value of the Working Income Supplement as it was in June 1998, calculated based on $11,200 annual income.

Figure 4: Both Family Income Plan and social assistance historical caseload series are from internal Saskatchewan Social Services sources. FIP is annual average for the fiscal year ending March 31 of the year indicated; social assistance is annual average for the calendar year.

Figure 5: Data series are Statistics Canada Low-Income Cut-offs before-tax on the 1992 base for individuals sixty-five or over and children under eighteen.

Figure 6: Federal and provincial programs are displayed using a tax and transfer model developed by the author. Program relationships should be considered approximate because there are differences in income definitions among these programs as well differences in accounting periods. Social assistance benefits, for example, are based on estimated current month's net income, while CCTB and SCB benefits are based on previous year's income as reported on Line 236 of income tax returns, which includes social assistance and certain other transfer payments.

Figure 7: Source: Author's tax and transfer model.
Figure 8: Source: Author's tax and transfer model.

Notes

1. Families reporting both positive and negative self-employment income in either reference year were excluded from this analysis. Exclusion of the self-employed helps deal with confounding effects on income distribution analysis caused by reported negative incomes of the self-employed.

2. While some might suggest addressing this problem through lower welfare tax-backs, this is not really a viable option. Earnings exemptions have the effect of raising the income threshold under which a family still qualifies for welfare. In Saskatchewan's pre-reform assistance regime, for example, a single parent with two children might qualify for the equivalent of about $14,000 per year in basic support, but because of earnings exemptions the family would still be on welfare at earned income levels of about $17,000. If the program used a more generous tax-back, such as 50 percent, the same family could still qualify for welfare at earnings of over $21,000 per year. This would significantly expand the cost and scope of welfare because it would entitle many more working families. It would also push the "reach" of the tax rate up to a level where it overlaps even more with income taxes and other benefit tax-backs, with negative effects on incentives for the working poor.

3. The Refundable Child Tax Credit, along with several child tax measures and the remnants of the universal family allowance, was replaced in 1993 by the federal Child Tax Benefit. This program has evolved, through the National Child Benefit initiative, into the current Canada Child Tax Benefit, an income-tested supplement program for low and middle-income families with an added tier of income support benefits for low-income families.

4. Because they compare each applicant's needs to available resources, social assistance programs are called "needs-tested" programs. The process of assessing needs also requires welfare administrations to review personal circumstances, which contributes to administrative overhead, intrusiveness and stigma. The "income-tested" approach is simpler and less personal. Benefits for a given family composition are based on income alone, not individual needs or circumstances. Income-tested programs are not as accurate at meeting each applicant's needs, but are administratively more efficient, and generally preferred by clients to the more "hands-on" approach of welfare.

5. Canada does not have an official "poverty line," but journalists and some analysts use LICOs as a proxy. Although the LICO has a number of problems as a national poverty measurement—most notably its unresponsiveness to regional variations in living costs—the LICO is a reasonable benchmark for measuring change over time. This time period represents the period for which this particular income measure has been available.

6. Only 231 senior individuals or senior-headed families qualified for social assistance in Saskatchewan in June 1998, on a total base of over 35,000 cases.

7. According to census counts, there were just over 19,000 "lone parents" in Saskatchewan in 1976 (Census of Canada, 1976), and 35,000 in 1996 (Census of Canada 1996)—about an 85 percent increase. While the census definition of a lone parent differs slightly from most common uses of the term "single parent," the trend is clear enough.

8. All provinces and territories except Québec participate directly in the NCB process. The Québec government claims exclusive jurisdiction over social programs, but has expressed agreement with NCB principles. Québec families benefit from NCB improvements to federal child benefit programs, and Québec's own child benefit reforms are consistent with those undertaken within the National Child benefit framework *per se*.

9. The speed and extent to which the NCB Supplement replaces provincial/territorial welfare depends on a number of factors in each jurisdiction's program design, in particular the rates paid for children's basic needs. These vary quite widely across the country. In parts of Canada where welfare rates are lowest, the NCB Supplement will more quickly overtake children's welfare. Children in these areas will benefit first from the rising national standard for child income security.

10. An earlier example of this type of program substitution is the Provincial Training Allowance (PTA), initiated by the Post-Secondary Education and Skills Training department of the Saskatchewan government in 1997. This program takes trainees out of welfare in favour of a program which is more clearly oriented towards training for work.

11. For example, the maximum basic federal benefit per child in June 1998 was $85 per month, and the net maximum welfare benefit $125.12, for a total of $210.12 per month. In July 1998 the federal benefit increased to $135.42 for the first child in a family. Provincial welfare no longer pays a benefit for children, but the Saskatchewan Child Benefit provides $75, for a total of $210.42. All federal and provincial supplements and ancillary benefits for children remain in place after the changeover. The expectation is that the CCTB will continue to increase, and the SCB decrease, until the federal government has assumed full responsibility for children's income support.

12. Some caution is required in comparing SCB parameters with welfare, because the Canada Child Tax Benefit income definition, which also drives the SCB, includes social assistance paid in the previous year.

13. Social assistance to Status Indians living on Saskatchewan reserves is a federal responsibility, but welfare programs on reserves, by policy, mirror provincial rates and policies. When Saskatchewan decided to move child benefits out of welfare and implement the SCB, the federal government agreed to fund a parallel benefit which would be paid to reserve families. The rates, business rules and delivery mechanism are the same as for the Saskatchewan Child Benefit.

14. Saskatchewan provides, through its own administrative systems, a Child Benefit Adjustment program which ensures that families do not receive less from the integrated payment, under the same circumstances, than they would have from welfare. The SCB/NCBS payment is the same or greater for the vast majority of families, but the conversion from a welfare base to a tax system-related base creates exceptional circumstances which the Child Benefit Adjustment will address. Most situations arise because the federal system uses previous year's income to determine benefits, which may not be adequate for family needs in a

given month of the current year. The Child Benefit Adjustment process compares the combined federal/provincial child benefit with what the family would have received from the pre-reform system and pays the family the difference.

15. In its initial form, SES benefits begin to accrue when family gross earnings exceed $125 per month. The benefit is a percentage of earnings, ranging by number of children from 25–45 percent. Maximum benefits levels of $175 to $315 per month are reached at gross earnings of $825 per month, and begin to be taxed back at $1075 per month. Eligibility is exhausted at incomes ranging from $1,775 to $2,235 per month.

16. Prior to July 1997 the WIS was a maximum of $500 per family per year, or $41.76 per month. Benefits began at $3,750, reached a maximum at $10,000, and were taxed back between $20,921 and $25,921. In July 1997 the federal government increased the maximum WIS, as a transitional measure to the NCB Supplement, to $605 for the first child, $405 for the second, and $330 for the third and subsequent child.

17. Pre-reform social assistance used a complex earnings exemption formula: a flat-rate exemption of $50–125 per month based on family size, plus 20 percent of additional earnings up to a maximum exemption level, which again varied by family size, but never exceeded $250 per month for non-disabled clients. With the introduction of SES, families' first $125 per month only is exempt. The effect of the former percentage exemption is built into SES. The SES benefit yields a higher return to clients, and SES benefits extend well beyond the social assistance threshold.

18. The observation from the National Longitudinal Survey of Children and Youth is cited in Statistics Canada 1997e. Social assistance utilization among single parents is based on internal Saskatchewan Social Services analysis.

19. Social assistance supplementary health coverage in Saskatchewan varies with circumstances, but most recipients qualify for free dental services, eye examinations and basic eyeglasses, ambulance, chiropractic services and medical supplies, as well as free or very low-cost prescriptions.

20. Adult benefits are similar to those formerly offered through the Family Income Plan, and include free chiropractic services and eye examinations, and reduced consumer charges for prescriptions.

4

Caring in
a Globalizing Economy:
Single Mothers on Assistance[1]

Karen Swift and Michael Birmingham

For much of this century, Canadian social assistance programs have provided financial support to many poor single mothers and their children for at least some period of the child-rearing years. In the current climate of globalization, mothers receiving assistance are seeing their benefits reduced, their caring labour denigrated and their very entitlements threatened. They are increasingly exhorted to enter the paid workforce as a method of increasing both their economic and social status. In this chapter we explore the context of these events and relate them to experiences of single mothers on social assistance in providing care for their children. These discussions are employed as the basis for a critique of the proposed National Child Benefit (NCB), promoted as a tool for reducing the depth of child poverty and increasing labour force attachment of welfare recipients. We argue that the proposed policy does more to support the globalization of capital than to improve conditions for this population, and we conclude with principles for evaluating relevant social policy in the new millennium.

The Context of Caring

Historically, single mothers have been an awkward group for social policy makers. Before the turn of this century they received support from both charitable organizations and newly developing social welfare programs. Early in the century, single mothers were the subject of a much debated policy shift toward (grudging) government support, at least during their children's early years, in the form of mothers' pensions. As the century rolled on, something approaching entitlement emerged, with single mothers receiving higher amounts of money, if still well below the poverty line, through social assistance and more benefits. At the same time, many barriers to entitlement eased in the second half of the century.

This progression toward continually improving social entitlements, which had come to seem like a fact of life, has taken a different turn in the 1990s. During this decade we have been introduced to the concept of "globalization," which refers to the ability of transnational corporations to move capital and jobs around the world to sites of greatest profitability. This "globalizing" world economy has simultaneously brought rhetoric about increasing the "productivity" of the labour force in order to enhance Canada's competitive position in world markets. Also during this decade the public has become convinced that the country suffers from a huge deficit which can only be eliminated through drastic cuts to social programs. These two trends are of course related, for Canada's competitive position can supposedly be improved by reducing both its deficit and the social costs for capital seeking profitable sites. In these endeavours neo-liberal politicians have taken the lead in promoting social policies that articulate Canadian resources to world competition and markets. The result has been reduction and dismantling of Canada's social safety net.

Certainly, Canadian single mothers and their children are at high risk of poverty in the 1990s. Female lone parents represent nearly half (47 percent) of poor non-elderly families with children, but constitute only 20 percent of this population (Hunsley 1996). Canada is in fact among the three highest Western countries in its poverty rate for single mothers, along with Australia and the United States. Although less than 10 percent of single mothers in some European countries are poor (Freiler and Cerny 1998), recent figures show that 61.4 percent of Canadian single mothers with children under eighteen live in poverty. This translates into 390,000 families. In the single parent mothers under age 25 the percentage in poverty rises to an unacceptable 91.3 percent (NCW 1998b:35). And as Hunsley (1996) notes, these mothers often find themselves in the lower strata of the poor. For these families, the decreasing entitlements, resources and security heralded by globalization and restructuring of the safety net are matters of considerable concern.

For a number of years attacks on welfare programs have been gaining strength and momentum. As Fraser (1989) has pointed out, this "welfare war" is largely about—and perhaps against—women. Single mothers are often particularly mentioned as a "target" for program cuts. While most Canadian policymakers are not willing to go to the lengths proposed by American neo-conservatives (e.g. Gingrich 1995), there has been a sharp shift in Canadian policy directions regarding vulnerable populations, including single mothers. This shift is toward lowering payments and reducing programs and benefits, while increasing pressure on women to consider moving from welfare to work. In reality, though only 44 percent of Canadian single mothers are represented in the welfare population, a much lower rate than in some comparable countries. In Australia, for example, 94 percent of single mothers receive assistance. In New Zealand the percentage is 89, and in the UK 79 percent of single mothers receive assistance (Baker 1998).

Benefits for all Canadian welfare recipients are below the poverty line. Depending on the province, single mothers on assistance receive from 48 to 69 percent of the official low income cut-off (LICO), figures that although quite low were established before substantial benefit reductions in Alberta and Ontario (Conway 1997; Freiler and Cerny 1998). Single mothers on assistance are also increasingly subject to scrutiny of their social contributions, labour and personal lives. Policy proposals such as "workfare" and training programs suggest that these women should no longer be seen as automatically entitled to financial support during child-rearing years but rather should be seen as costly and unproductive people who would be better regarded as potential recruits for the labour market, an idea captured in the phrase "moving women from welfare to work."

At the same time, important shifts in Canada's employment picture are occurring. Recently reported figures from Statistics Canada (1997a) show the unemployment rate, although down from 1996, continuing at quite a high level—8.6 percent as of December 1997. This translates into more than 1.3 million unemployed Canadians. The unemployment rate is decreasing more significantly for men than for women. Figures show male unemployment down from 10 percent at year end 1996, to 8.6 percent at the end of 1997. Unemployment for women in the same period decreased from 9.5 percent to 8.5 percent. This translates into 89,000 more new jobs for Canadian men than for women in 1997. Part-time jobs, although slightly decreasing over 1997 as a percentage of all jobs, remain a significant part of overall employment at 18.5 percent of employment.

It is important to note that women have gained ground in employment over the past several decades largely in the public and quasi-public arenas—for instance teaching and nursing—which are now the targets of budget-cutting exercises. This trend means not only loss of good jobs for women, but entails devolving caring labour from areas of full-time paid work to "the community." Announcements of massive hospital closings and school restructurings quite commonly include vague suggestions that "community care," "home care," volunteerism, personal involvement and "family care" are superior ways to deliver most services requiring personal care. Some of this care will undoubtedly be assumed by lower paid, lower skilled workers, mostly women, as home care workers, homemakers, nurse's aides, tutors, etc. Clearly, much of the work of personal care now being de-institutionalized and de-budgeted will also devolve onto the shoulders of unpaid women in the private home.

Politicians at both the federal and provincial levels have stressed creation of new jobs as central to their plans for revitalizing the economy.

Such political rhetoric generally includes the need for training programs. "It doesn't take a rocket scientist," according to Paul Martin, federal Finance Minister, "to know you've got to do a lot more training" (Quoted in *Toronto Star* March 8, 1997:A1). It remains unclear what this training will be *for*, given the current high unemployment rate and dire predictions that this rate may be here to stay. As Baker's (1998) research shows, efforts to increase employability are expensive; however, politicians usually avoid making generous commitments to training programs. In any case, experience in other Western countries demonstrates that labour force participation does not help many single mothers stay out of poverty (Freiler and Cerny 1998). In Canada, many employed single mothers, like their counterparts on welfare, can expect to be poor, since they earn on average only 38 percent of incomes that two parent families earn (Hunsley 1996). Moreover, some American analysts are suggesting that workfare policies could further erode wages for the poorest third of the population, which certainly includes many single mothers (Swanson 1998).

To summarize, both material support and entitlements of Canadian single mothers on social assistance, already ungenerous in relation to other industrialized countries, are under threat in the new world of globalization, and these women are frequently urged to improve their position by "getting back to work." At the same time, earnings of single mothers in the workforce are quite low, and women's work generally is being de-skilled, devalued and devolved. Women who do paid labour will be paid less, and will likely have less secure jobs requiring less education and training. At home, women are expected to take on more caring labour, some of it the skilled labour previously done by paid professionals. Frequently missing from the discussion is the question of how the most vulnerable women, including single mothers, are to support and provide care for their children in this developing scenario.

Caring Labour and Need

The idea of caring as it has been developed primarily by feminists is used to conceptualize elements of relational life as experienced by women. Women are usually involved in personal relationships with others as part of their everyday lives; whereas men's lives often focus on manipulating objects or events. Caring can be seen not as a separate sphere of life at all, but as pervasive in women's lives (Fisher and Tronto 1990), which may help to explain its invisibility. Traditionally, caring has been seen as a natural and positive aspect of women's lives, as what they are "naturally" suited for. This happy view has been challenged by feminists who point to the burdens and labour that caring imposes on women (Noddings 1984; Graham 1983).

In Western society labour is generally noticed and valued only when it is paid labour. Many social analysts have explored how the gendered division between home and paid work developed in relation to capitalist modes of production (see Vellekoop-Baldock 1990, for example). As women were increasingly consigned to the private sphere, their domestic labour became invisible and defined as outside the "productive" process. This dichotomy has of course continued into the present, as has the moral value clearly attached to paid work. Processes through which unpaid work is distributed are hidden, as is the entire arena of unpaid caring labour which involves acts of concern for others not accounted for in the "work ethic" model. Thus, "work" has come to be synonymous with paid labour. Even the single mothers participating in our research, after outlining a prodigious amount of labour done in the home, lamented the fact that they weren't "working."

Single mothers must act as both breadwinners and as caregivers, which is one reason they pose a problem for policy-makers as well as for ideologues. The difficulty of meshing these responsibilities does not fit the dichotomized view of a person either working or not working. Beginning with the idea of "mother's pensions" earlier in the century, various proposals for breaching this contradiction by compensating mothers for their caring labour have been put forward. Currently, though, welfare or social assistance is conceptualized not as a form of breadwinning, but as a condition of "dependence" on the state. Further, receipt of social assistance is increasingly cast as involving no actual work. Welfare itself has come to be seen as a barrier or disincentive to "real work," so much so that some commentators have begun referring to social assistance as the "welfare wall" (Caledon Institute 1997).

The notion of caring labour is closely related to and in fact rooted in "need" (Fisher and Tronto 1990). Ideas concerning need come mostly from male-dominated domains such as philosophy and public policy and centre upon differentiating what is essential to us from what we merely desire. This distinction is important in the public world because need distinguishes which of our desires entitles us to the resources of others; simple desire, on the other hand, is "capricious" (Thompson 1987:98) and unfettered by social obligations (Ignatieff 1984).

The discourse of need also addresses itself to defining different kinds of need, distinguishing for instance survival needs from the need to flourish (Ignatieff 1984; Doyal and Gough 1991). Marx differentiated between "natural needs," those physical needs required to be met for continued existence, and "necessary needs," which are natural needs plus a sense of normalcy (Heller 1976). Recently, the notion of needs as "thick" and "thin" has been developed by Fraser (1989), one of the few women recognized as contributing a conception of need. A thin need is objective and universal, while thick needs are understood and interpreted in cultural context and relate to the quest for development and fulfilment. The idea of "thick" needs echoes Marx' conceptualization of need as multifaceted and positive. Marx in fact spoke of need as wealth—a person "rich in needs" was a "human being in need of a totality of human manifestations of life" (quoted in Heller 1976:143–4). In 1990s Canada, however, discussions of need are far from this conception. Increasingly in the social and political domain, "need" is limited to "natural" need—the most basic requirements of survival. This narrow (and neo-liberal) definition of need justifies minimal claims on the public purse and therefore fits the agenda of deficit reduction. Currently at issue is whether the need to "flourish," to be fulfilled, or to feel socially "normal" constitute any claims on the public purse.

Contemporary social policy debates centre upon determining not only what will qualify as needs but also on determining systems of obligation for meeting various needs. The development of the liberal welfare state represented an attempt to increase society's obligation to meet the needs of its members, and to move some obligations from individual families and the community to the social whole. The very existence of the welfare state normalizes the condition of need and tends to reduce moral judgements of the needs expressed by individuals and families. With the shift to neo-liberal politics, however, the obligation for meeting need is devolving back from the state to family and community. As the liberal welfare state has dwindled, social claims are being reduced to "natural" or survival need as the only legitimate social claim: "Sure you try to make your food last," one mother told us. "I eat, but I don't eat as much as I used to because I can't afford it."

The Lived Experience of Caring

As part of our research, three focus groups[2] were organized to explore with single mothers on welfare their experiences and perceptions. The women in all three groups were asked to discuss their perceptions of what they and their children need, the labour involved in trying to meet these needs and their relationships to welfare and the larger society. In this chapter we do not attempt to generalize findings, but rather we employ the open-ended discussion of these mothers to make visible specific aspects of caring for children. However, the personal and financial situations of these women are typical of other similar women in Canada and the United States, an assertion supported by reference to literature concerning single mothers on assistance (Ellwood 1988; Davis and Hagen 1996; Ozawa 1994; Rank 1994; Lindsey 1994; Kitchen and Popham 1998). Mothers' understanding of their situations demonstrates common issues, problems, solutions and possibilities for women in similar circumstances.

The lived experience of caring for children in circumstances of small and shrinking resources reflects neither neo-liberal conceptions of need nor many of the theoretical concepts and categories used to describe need. There is in fact little in contemporary discourse that adequately captures the experience of mothers' attempts to meet needs with minimal resources. As we will see, the labour involved in determining and meeting the needs of children is considerably more immediate, complex, contradictory, "messy" and painful than suggested by most contemporary ideology and discourse. Mothers describe a barrage of different, often conflicting, upsetting and impossible demands conveyed to them by their children and by others in contact with their children. They describe children screaming, demanding and even leaving home over their inability to provide for needs and wants.

In general, these women stated the needs of their families in strikingly modest terms: "I want my kid to be able to open the fridge door and have whatever he wants." Of course, mothers on assistance must understand and address themselves to the crucial problem of meeting survival needs: "Food is my first priority, bills are my second priority. Then I have to worry about boots and coats for winter," said one mother. Another "decided not to pay the [Hydro] bill and concentrate on food." However, statements suggest that what might now be construed as mere desire, mothers often experience as essential to the well-being of their children. "I had to borrow a dollar to put under his pillow [for the tooth fairy]."

Certainly, the children of these mothers do not accept the neo-liberal view of need as mere survival. As one of the mothers pointed out, children compare themselves to others. They "see their peers wearing better clothes, [eating] better school lunches and some have tutors who teach them at home." Another agreed: "Teenage children like to wear good clothes because they want to have what other teenagers have. We (single mothers) can't afford to buy what they need anymore."

While categorizations of need may help to guide policy, they miss the labour and emotional costs of trying to meet need. These mothers eat less, put off buying clothes for themselves—even winter coats—beg from friends and lovers and are torn by what they cannot provide in their needs-meeting efforts. For one, guilt followed her departure from an abusive relationship which had allowed her child to have some of the "normal" possessions of a Canadian child: "He had a Nintendo, he had two bikes. Because I couldn't live with the abuse anymore, I took my kid away from this and he doesn't have this anymore. If I stayed there and got beat up every day, my kid would still have everything."

This mother's anguished statement reveals a critical characteristic of need, often missing from philosophical and policy discussions, which is the economic context in which needs emerge. It is in the very nature of capitalism that new needs and thus new markets are continually created. Canadians are encouraged and taught that spending and purchasing spurs economic growth, based on the assumption that "when a dollar changes hands, economic growth occurs" (Hawken 1997:48). In capitalist economies, and even more so in a globalizing world economy, it becomes almost a duty of the citizen to purchase up-to-date goods and services. Seldom are the social qualities and benefits of goods and services questioned in this discourse. Mothers, including single mothers, accept the idea that they should be "proper" consumers, providing fast food and computer games for their young. Children themselves become advocates for new and trendy products and put pressure on their mothers to meet their "need" to be like their peers. Mothers express the contradictory pressures on them to be proper consumers with the substantially contracting resources available to them: "I'd love to go out and take my son to McDonald's, but I can't afford to …. It tears my heart out to tell that little boy, 'No, Mommy can't afford it.'" Low-income mothers in capitalist society, in other words, are under constant pressure to view what neo-liberals now construe to be "desires" as the normal and necessary needs of children. It is the pressure of this contradiction that is intended to drive them off welfare and into the paid labour force.

Current rhetoric about single mothers on assistance is that they are "not working." These mothers, however, report a substantial amount of labour involved in meeting needs of their children at home. This labour was captured in the phrase "24/7", meaning they see themselves as being on duty twenty-four hours a day, seven days a week. As one reasonably pointed out, "there's no one else to do it." Strenuous efforts and labour are involved in efforts to meet children's needs: mothers attempt to extract resources from various government programs, make trips across town to more generous food banks, engage in political action to change laws, take small jobs, trade child care, organize community suppers, skip meals, plan purchases to take advantage of bulk rates, borrow food and money, make personal and legal approaches to fathers of their children and budget their money many months in advance.

Since Ontario's 21 percent reduction in welfare benefits, the labour of feeding and clothing their children has increased for all of these mothers, and especially for those in market housing, since their rent now consumes a much larger portion of their total income. Shopping takes longer, in order to "shop the specials." More trips to food banks and clothing depots were reported, and considerably more time is spent juggling different bills, trying to figure out how much to pay on each without incurring too much penalty. These mothers also spend considerable time and effort to find information about benefits they might be able to qualify for and on making comparisons of different kinds of benefits available to various subgroups of mothers on welfare. Our focus groups, in fact, provided an occasion for some of this information to be shared.

The neo-liberal agenda calls for "training" mothers on assistance, along with others, in order to increase their participation in the labour force. This proposal is generally understood to imply that mothers on welfare are unskilled. At work here is the notion of caring as "natural," an activity flowing from love that requires none of the special learning or skill that are cast as the attributes of paid labour. Mothers in our focus groups did not at all accept the notion that caring labour requires no special skill. In fact, they saw professional "roles" in their caring labour: doctor, nurse, accountant, speech therapist, counsellor, cook, mediator, social worker, public speaker, therapist. Some women are adamant that their skills were no different from those of professionals paid to do the same work. One mother described her work as a "speech therapist" for her son:

> Speech pathologist(s) make a lot of money. I'm ... doing the exact same things as what they're doing and what they're telling me to do with my son; it's the same thing. I think that the work that single mothers do at home is the same as any professional out there working.

Another described how she approaches "therapy" with children under stress:

> Once you get them past the anger and you start really going down deep into their feelings, you have to focus on them, you have to talk to them. It may take you ten minutes, it may take you hours ... with my son ... other kids pick on him about his weight .... If he went to a therapist or whatever, this hour session would cost something like $100.

In addition, many of these women are educated and have skill training and experience in various kinds of paid employment. Also striking are the kinds and depth of volunteer activities reported by these mothers, including advocacy work, public speaking on behalf of social and economic issues, planning and execution of needs assessment surveys and program development and co-ordination. Volunteer activity was the source of considerable esteem-building as well as skill development for some women:

> When we did the park, I co-ordinated the whole child care part. I had two assistants with me. I never thought I could pull it through. I couldn't believe that I did it. I said to myself: "Hey, I did this."

A common contemporary image of single mothers on welfare is that they are "sitting at home and waiting for the cheque," an image well known to mothers in our groups and in fact articulated by several of them. Underlying this idea is a justification for moving mothers off welfare and into the labour market: they are a social cost and a group that makes no social contribution. However, the single mothers in our groups are not sitting at home. Through their caring labour they contribute to the economy in a variety of ways. Further, their work is not confined to the private realm; rather a constant flow between public and private spheres characterizes the lives of both the mothers and their children. Mothers conduct aspects of their caring labour in the world of commercial enterprise, as well as in government offices, schools and classrooms, community centres and recreation sites. Not only are these mothers performing labour with and on behalf of their children in the public sphere, they also spend money, participate in the exchange and distribution of goods, create networks and facilitate connections with other community members, provide direct and unpaid care for friends, relatives and neighbours, build and sustain volunteer services and provide and receive all kinds of services. In short, they help to create and sustain the social and economic fabric. In addition, mothers perform valuable reproductive labour in socializing their children to become punctual, educated and appropriate workers. The labour performed by these mothers, as by any other consumers, acts to stimulate the economy, helping to create and sustain employment in for-profit businesses as well as non-profit services.

Many of the mothers in our groups were also involved in a variety of working and reciprocal relations with other people. They described babysitting trade-offs, joint cooking sessions, door-to-door surveys, participation in community meetings, development of community groups and networks and sister-like friendships. A few had agenda books to keep track of their many activities. These relationships suggest an array of "people skills" that usually go unnoticed, which include making and sustaining relationships, engaging in reciprocity and sharing, supporting others, organizing groups and practising effective communications and advocacy skills.

Nevertheless, women feel the stigma of welfare in powerful ways. One woman in our study expressed the feeling this way:

> It's so disrespected that you're a single parent at home .... People see me as one of the deadbeats out there who's on social assistance. Well, I'm sorry. I'm degraded. I just try to hold up my head and walk straight and do my daily thing.

This comment brings attention to the class contradictions embedded in this stigma. On the one hand it is not seen as socially acceptable for mothers on assistance to care for their children full time at home. On the other hand, middle- and upper-middle-class women are often encouraged to remain out of the workforce during their children's younger years if at all possible. Caring labour, it appears, is not evenly devalued; it is the caring labour of *particular* mothers, those in receipt of public resources, that is viewed as socially expendable.

A number of women in our groups have previously been in the paid labour force and several expressed strong desires to re-enter the workforce. Mothers in all groups indicated they would like the opportunity to "work." "I'd sooner have a full-time job than stay home." The problem, of course, is that the caring labour these women provide, while absolutely essential, is mostly invisible, easy to ignore, and socially unvalued; consequently it quickly disappears from policy and planning efforts. There are also a substantial number of structural barriers to mothers' labour-force partici-pation. Employment status in the country, the absence of accessible child care, a large number of young children to care for, inadequate transporta-tion, special needs of children and potential loss of benefits allowed through the welfare system were just a few of those mentioned in focus groups.

Like recent American studies (Davis and Hagan 1996) this research suggests that single mothers who rely on social assistance often believe they are productive and have a right to be compensated for their reproduc-tive labour. They believe that the welfare system has the responsibility to provide support as long as they are working to better their own lives, the lives of their children and the lives of others living in their community. Their sense of entitlement is seen in relation to their caring labour for children. Similar to other studies (Rank 1994; Davis and Hagan 1996) the respondents externalize their reasons for being on welfare. They see themselves as having little control over either the circumstances that placed them on welfare or the circumstances that continue to keep them there, although they hold out hope that their situations will eventually change. While some women saw themselves getting "real" work in the future when they were free of child care responsibilities, others still hoped to meet a man.

Mothers' responses to questions about caring labour point to impor-tant issues that could and should be reflected in policy proposals. One is that it is erroneous to say that single mothers on assistance are not working. Meeting needs involves complex activities of planning, research, strategizing, visualizing, anticipating, budgeting, relationship building, advocacy, questioning, listening and attending, doing for, doing with and "being with." For single mothers on assistance, these activities constitute a substantial workload, requiring many skills. In fact, their high levels of poverty demand coping and management skills that wealthier Canadians need never develop. The experiences reported by these mothers also suggest that considerable skilled caring labour is already being done on an unpaid basis, often by those with the fewest resources. Further, dominant neo-liberal discourse is contradictory in suggesting that needs for public purposes are mere survival while needs for economic purposes "require" a continual flow of new products and services. This contradiction presents substantial labour for low-income mothers, as they attempt to mediate socially produced consumption needs with a public view of need as mere survival. Finally, it appears that caring labour is more highly valued when it is privately rather than publicly financed.

The "Welfare Wall" and NCB

In the face of a globalizing economy and a neo-liberal social policy agenda, how can the real life experiences and the profound poverty of many single mothers on assistance be addressed? Many social advocates, of course, would like to see the welfare state rebuilt and strengthened. Feminists might well respond to this solution by questioning whether equity has ever actually existed, given the basic inequities built into the welfare state at the outset (Fraser 1989). As Leira (1994:198) argues, the full range of rights and entitlements offered by the welfare state have never been equally available to women. This is because the system of entitlements is based on the organization of labour in industrial capitalism, which gives preference to formal employment over other forms of work more often done by women. What matters in this scheme is not the hours worked, the years committed or the societal significance of the tasks performed, but the formal work contract and the wage.

The neo-liberal approach to poverty is "workfare," an approach requiring that those "able" to enter the paid labour force, including single mothers, provide "approved" labour in return for social assistance payments. Critics of this policy are legion, of course. Schragge (1997:33) views workfare as a "punitive response to wider changes in the structures of the economy and in work ... [promoted] partly in an attempt to prove that work remains a possibility." From an entitlement point of view, Pascal (1993) forcefully argues against the notion that rights imply duties, including caregiving duties, noting that mere redefinition of duty can cost women their entitlements in such a scheme. Taken to its logical conclusion, even the most basic needs of able-bodied adults and their dependent children might not constitute legitimate claims for entitlement. Many women, however, closely connect their caring labour with social entitlement.

For many people, the most acceptable approach for addressing the poverty of Canada's children is the proposed National Child Benefit. Through this policy, federal and provincial income security programs would be integrated, becoming a single benefit paid to all low-income families with dependent children. Three main objectives for the benefit are claimed. These include "preventing and reducing the depth of child poverty, promoting attachment to the workforce ... and reducing overlap and duplication of child-related benefits" (Battle and Mendelson 1997). The model is promoted by prominent social policy experts as an important first step in alleviating poverty and equalizing benefits among low-income families. Among its advantages are that it simplifies income support, that it will be income- rather than needs-tested, and that it will provide portability so that families moving into low-wage jobs from welfare will not lose the benefit. Proponents of this policy shift note that it is designed to reduce rather than "cure" poverty (Battle and Mendelson 1997:2), and that it will reduce the "fairness" gap between families on assistance and the working poor, whose children at present may be even more poverty-stricken than those whose parents receive welfare (Caledon Institute 1997). It is clear, however, that part of the rationale for this approach is the reduction of disincentives to labour force participation by women on welfare. This proposal, in other words, is intended to begin bringing down the "welfare wall" that supposedly stands between individuals and the paid labour force.

In its favour, the proposed National Child Benefit attempts to address some of the issues raised by mothers themselves. The plan does recognize the importance of meeting children's needs regardless of the situation of their parents. It also has the potential to simplify the benefit system, hopefully reducing the labour some mothers are currently performing in order to obtain all available benefits. It might also address some of the inequities among the different populations represented in our three focus groups, and it might eventually decrease, at least slightly, the depth of their poverty. As well, it has at least the potential to allow low-income single mothers to participate in the labour force on some basis of interest, skill development and need for extra money without penalizing them with loss of benefits for their children. It might also reduce the scrutiny and shame mothers on welfare experience.

However, the particular situations of mothers on assistance also suggest some problems with this proposal. The very idea of a welfare wall assumes that it is primarily the structure of welfare that leads women to withdraw from or never enter the paid labour force. This construction renders the very substantial caring labour of single mothers on welfare even less visible than it has previously been. The welfare wall idea hides the fact that these mothers are at home because they *are* working. They are engaging, as our groups clearly demonstrate, in substantial, complex, skilled, important and necessary social labour. The proposal, while implicitly devaluing caring labour, fails to explain how this absolutely essential work will be done if mothers move into the labour force. The impending demands on this same population of mothers for additional caring responsibility, in the form of "community care," also disappear in the formulation and promotion of the National Child Benefit.

The welfare wall idea also suggests that some of the previously accepted public responsibility for addressing the needs of vulnerable populations can and should be devolved back onto the shoulders of individual parents. In promoting and defending the policy, Battle and Mendelson (1997), for example, frequently mention the importance of "the private family" and of encouraging parents' primary responsibility for children. Although the proposed benefit is potentially more generous and stable than current welfare programs, the language used to support and promote it is the language of neo-liberal social policy. The neo-liberal approach, as various analysts make clear (O'Neill 1998), is designed to present Canada as an "investor-friendly" country that has streamlined its social spending and developed policies reducing disincentives to join the paid labour force. In the process of promoting this image, notions of social and public responsibility for citizens and residents in need, once enshrined in the values of the welfare state, give way to the neo-liberal ideology of individualism. Further, the model allows for the definitive separation of public responsibilities for children from the adults who care for them. The approach allows the federal government the appearance of addressing child poverty at the same time as it takes a tough stand against welfare.

This policy proposal also fits well with the shape of the "new" job market of part-time insecure work. As proponents note (Battle and Mendelson 1997), the proposed approach allows people to move back and forth from the labour force to assistance with minimum penalty. In this respect, the policy is well suited and perhaps even specifically designed to support and enhance the potential for low-wage, contract work that characterizes the operations of transnational corporations (Korten 1995). In effect, the policy helps to cement a new state-corporate partnership, which both reflects and encourages the kinds of employment likely to be offered to many Canadians—or to others—we are encouraged to fear, if Canadians do not refit themselves to compete. In this new welfare system corporate interests are served through the potential for new populations of low-wage workers being made available in a flexible way, which current welfare systems simply do not allow, thus reducing the threat of social instability in the event of substantial job loss. This arrangement also encourages capital investment by effectively subsidizing corporate costs of labour. In this scheme low-wage, short-term jobs for parents will be subject to less criticism as the cause of child poverty. For its part, the

Canadian state benefits by improving its "look" as a promising place for capital to invest.

Another benefit to the Canadian economy is the warm-up, cool-down effect of the child benefit, mentioned by advocates of the proposal:

> Because the new National child Benefit System is geared to income, more will go to families whose income is falling in bad economic times, and they will spend the income, helping the economy to recover. Conversely, when the economy improves, incomes should go up and child benefits to low-income families should in total decrease relative to the economy as a whole, thereby decreasing demand for goods and services and helping to cool off the economy. (Battle and Mendelson 1997)

This rationale at least acknowledges and legitimizes our earlier sugges-tion—mothers on welfare are not simply receivers at the public purse. In fact, low-income populations and the social programs they use for support are necessary economic tools that can be and are used to adjust economic trends in a globalizing economy.

For women currently on assistance, this proposal will likely do them and their children little good, at least at the beginning. This is because the current plan would allow provinces to reduce the assistance levels of recipients by the amount of their federally financed child benefit. Thus, they would be no better off with the benefit, at least in the first phase of implementation. The rationale for this decision is that it will equalize the benefits for the working poor, thus reducing the "fairness gap" and mak-ing a start at chipping away at the "welfare wall" (Battle and Mendelson 1997). In reality, as Freiler (1997) notes, the working poor are really the beneficiaries. The main benefit of this plan for single mothers on assist-ance, then, is to encourage them into the paid labour force where they may be able to keep some of the wages they earn. For those who cannot enter the labour force, current poverty levels will prevail. The failure to benefit welfare recipients who, for the most part, are single mothers, indirectly reinforces traditional two-parent family structures. This "tough love" approach is in fact recommended by some observers (C.D. Howe Institute *Communique* January 14, 1998) as a method of reducing the number of mother-led families.

Alternative Directions

To conclude, we propose a number of principles against which social policy directions in the new millennium, including the National Child Benefit, should be judged. First, policies must transcend market and profit values. The overwhelming discourse of globalization has all but silenced the language of human development and non-material values. The state, once the centre of social policy development, is increasingly driven by market forces. To the extent that this occurs, the possibilities for human growth and health for all but the most wealthy will diminish.

The generously given comments and stories of women in our focus groups reflect efforts of mothers to assert themselves as people "rich in needs," people trying to fulfil and express a broad range of human experience. In so doing, they expose their children to much more than market-driven needs and values. Of course, these very low-income mothers express needs for increased material support, and policy directions must include the alleviation of poverty as a crucial objective. We argue, however, that policies designed to address the needs of low-income groups must recognize and acknowledge not simply survival needs but the "thick" human and social needs of people to flourish. The profit motive, which would appear as the only goal and benefit of transnational corporate structures, certainly cannot provide guidance in this respect. It falls then to the state, to the community and to individuals to ensure that our shared social life and policies are infused with a spirit of generosity and belief in more than profit motives. In this, we might well be guided by the mothers in our study, whose lived reality reflects values beyond mere profit. The National Child Benefit does make a modest beginning at recognizing that the needs of children should be viewed as a social entitlement. However, the same recognition is not extended to their caregivers. In our view, an acceptable benefit would be one that acknowledges entitlement on grounds of a humanitarian interest in human development for both adults and children.

Second, we argue, along with others, for a principle of public responsibility for children that is universally applied. The National Child Benefit does take the first step in meeting this criterion. However, proponents of the plan back away from any concept of universality (Battle and Mendelson, 1997). In the climate of globalization it has become popular to suggest that universal social programs are too expensive and therefore unrealistic. However, it is important to remember that transnational corporations seek sites of low social cost and demand. If they are successful in persuading welfare states to abandon commitments to their populations, not only the children of the poor but those of the middle class will lose health benefits, educational opportunities and social access. Universalism, therefore, remains a value against which social programs should be evaluated.

Third, in addition to making visible the needs of children, social policies must make visible the primary means of meeting these needs, which is caring labour. This labour not only addresses the needs of children, but builds a healthier community for all of us. The National Child Benefit does not recognize or value this labour. Acceptable social policies will ensure that caring labour is made visible and in turn valued, supported and compensated by society. A benefit built on this principle will help to redistribute wealth rather than simply reaffirming existing class and gender structures.

A fourth criterion for social policy is that the interests of mothers and children should not be divided. One of our major concerns with the proposed National Child Benefit is its contradictory goals of reducing child poverty and removing women from welfare. In effect, children are going to receive additional entitlements from the federal government while their mothers may be increasingly disentitled by provincial governments, an approach that acknowledges children's needs while potentially ignoring the needs and contributions of their mothers. We argue that a humane and appropriate policy will not position children and mothers so radically differently in relation to the state. An acceptable policy would recognize that the needs of children of single mothers can be better met by fully functioning mothers whose own needs are respected and accounted for.

Fifth, new policy should reduce the effects of stigma and social marginalization felt by recipients. Mothers in our study expressed enormous emotion about the shame they felt and the shaming practices that appear endemic to welfare programs. The National Child Benefit does recognize and address this issue. However, the direction of the policy is to reduce stigma through entry into the job market. Given the many and substantial barriers mothers experience in entering the labour force, most of which are not addressed in the proposed benefit, it is doubtful that many of them will be able to move off welfare as a result of this policy. It is questionable whether the unstable and low-wage jobs many mothers can secure will lead to pride and increased labour force attachment. Further, there is nothing in the policy suggesting that the significant skills of these mothers are going to be socially or economically recognized, valued or compensated in the developing job market.

Finally, an important policy criterion is that different groups within the low-income population not be disadvantaged in relation to one another. Rather, policy should be an instrument to reduce disparities among social and economic classes. Proponents of the National Child Benefit (Battle and Mendelson 1997) rightly point out that working poor families have in many cases been disadvantaged in relation to families on assistance, and they promote the importance of eliminating this "fairness gap." However, rather than recognizing the needs of all families, the plan focuses on benefits for the working poor as its first priority, leaving single mothers on assistance in essentially the same position of poverty they currently occupy. If implemented as recommended by the Caledon Institute (1997), this policy would effectively reorganize relations within the poorest class, creating a new "fairness" gap favouring the working poor over those on assistance. The policy could also act indirectly to reinforce a traditional family value system while discouraging the single-mother model. There is already pressure from neo-liberal sources designed to encourage women, and in particular poor women, to move to traditional family structures (Richards 1998), a pressure based on the high rate of poverty among unattached women (NCW 1998b). Although less direct, the National Child Benefit appears to support the same goal.

We argue that to take the challenges of globalization seriously in the twenty-first century we must rethink our concept of "socially useful labour" and how we compensate this labour. The so-called third sector of non-government, non-profit organizations will plan an important role in this rethinking, for it is primarily in this arena that low paid and unpaid caring labour will be conceptualized and distributed. Liberal proponents of third sector strategies (Rifkin 1995; Segal 1997) focus on strategies designed to prop up capitalism, which in turn will facilitate globalizing trends. Rifkin (1995) recommends subsidizing the third sector through workfare and the guaranteed annual income in order to ensure that capitalism prospers even in the conditions of massive job loss. We, on the other hand, support third sector recommendations intended to promote healthier communities. Our research suggests that an important component of this project will be the redefinition of "work" in ways that include, value and fairly compensate caring labour.

In the current environment of high unemployment and shrinking remuneration for many, revised ideas about what people really need and how needs can best be met have important implications for the structure and meaning of caring labour. Presently, single mothers on assistance are caught in a maze of contradictory and apparently inescapable obligations which they cannot possibly meet. In a way, these mothers represent and symbolize the intolerable contradictions between globalizing capital and public obligation. In honourably and adequately addressing the problems they face in meeting the needs of their families and in being recognized as valued members of society, we may learn a great deal that will benefit the social whole.

Notes

1. The research carried out for this project would not have been possible without support of a SSHRC Network grant.
2. All three groups were organized in Ottawa. Group 1 involved Canadian-born women living in subsidized housing. Group 2 was composed of Canadian born mothers living in market housing, struggling financially because of the high cost of their housing relative to reduced welfare benefits. Group 3 was composed of Somali women who hold refugee status in Canada. This group was conducted by a Somali graduate student in the women's own language, and translated into English.

5

Child Poverty and the CCTB/NCB:
Why Most Poor Children Gain Nothing

Jane Pulkingham and Gordon Ternowetsky

In the last two years considerable attention has been devoted to the development of new policies designed to address the growing problem of poverty among families with children. In the 1997–98 federal budget, Paul Martin presented the much-publicized new Canada Child Tax Benefit (CCTB) (Canada 1997a). Later that year further details regarding this benefit and the role the provinces and territories would assume in its delivery were presented in a joint federal-provincial paper, *Working Together Towards a National Child Benefit* (Canada 1997b). In the 1998-99 federal budget a further $850 million was allocated for the CCTB/National Child Benefit (NCB). This is to be paid in two instalments—$450 million in July 1999 and the remainder in July 2000. The details regarding how these additional funds are to be allotted and administered by the provinces and territories still need to be clarified (Canada 1998b).

Common sense and the buildup leading to this new program of child benefits suggests that it will amount to more money for Canada's poor children. This would be a noble objective, but it is not realized. Careful examination shows that this new system of federal benefits is a misleading and seriously flawed method of enriching incomes for poor children. For example, child poverty advocates locate the problem of child poverty primarily as an issue of inadequate family income and the need to increase total family income (in part by means of an enhanced child benefit) regardless of the income source of parents. Federal and provincial governments crafted an agreement that will not improve the financial position of the poorest of poor children who come from families who receive income from provincial/territorial social assistance and who also constitute the majority of poor families with children. Rather, they have instituted a policy that fixes child benefit levels for income assistance recipients to the prevailing (and inadequate) levels of support they receive through income assistance and child benefits. Thus the new system continues the practice of legislating poverty for these children and their families. It also reinforces the requirement to work even when there are not enough jobs and those that do exist are increasingly low-paid. This requirement is particularly problematic for single parents who rely on income assistance while they look after their children. Finally, despite appearances, the new CCTB/NCB adds very little, if any, "new money" to existing federal–provincial income transfers for poor children.

Government rhetoric, framing the introduction of the new child benefit system, suggests that the policy is primarily intended to effect a reduction in child poverty. But the political debate and policy response to child poverty reveals that the new system is constructed largely around three other sets of problems. The first (and over-riding) is the assumption that reliance on income assistance (hence the poverty rate itself) is artificially inflated because recipients are generally unmotivated to undertake paid employment and require work incentives to move them into paid work. The second problem is the "welfare wall" or poverty trap faced by families who receive provincial income assistance or find themselves worse off when they undertake paid employment. This concerns the financial barriers faced by income assistance recipients in moving to paid employment because of the loss of in-kind benefits (e.g., health and dental coverage) and added work-related expenses (e.g., transportation costs, clothing and child care).[1] This is perceived to exacerbate the general tendency to be "welfare dependent" and "work shy." The third problem is the differential treatment of poor families who receive income assistance and those who do not, in terms of the total federal/provincial child income benefits that they receive. In some jurisdictions, combined federal/provincial income benefits directed at children are higher for income assistance recipients than working-poor families with equivalent incomes.

In addition to a reduction in child poverty, removing the welfare wall and providing equivalent levels of income support to children in families with equivalent incomes are important policy objectives. As the following analysis of the new system suggests, it is not clear that any of these objectives are met. On the contrary, they are largely negated by the over-riding concern to financially assist only those who "help themselves" by undertaking low paid work.

Below we examine the Child Tax Benefit (CTB) and Working Income Supplement (WIS) that constitute the former child benefit program upon which the recent CCTB/NCB initiatives are being built. In addition, we summarize and critique the changes in child benefits announced in the 1997 federal budget and the intergovernmental paper on the NCB. These changes are being implemented in two stages. Stage 1, began in July 1997, by increasing and restructuring the Work Income Supplement (WIS) component of the former Child Tax Benefit (CTB). Stage 2, started in July 1998, combines the enriched WIS and the CTB basic benefit into one payment to form the new CCTB/NCB.

Reforming the Child Tax Benefit

The CCTB and the WIS
Before July 1997 the CTB (including the WIS) amounted to federal expenditures of $5.1 billion annually. This consisted of the basic child benefit of $1,020 per child for families with incomes under $25,921. For families with three or more children, $75 was added to the basic child benefit of $1,020 per child for the third and subsequent children. Above the income cut-off of $25,921 benefit levels were reduced. In addition to this basic benefit, there was also the WIS. Prior to July 1997 it amounted to a flat rate benefit of $500 per year, per eligible family.

The CCTB/NCB: Stages 1 and 2
In July 1997 (Stage 1 of the CCTB) the WIS was changed to take into account the number of children in families. Benefits increased from $500 per family to $605 for the first child, $405 for the second and $330 for each additional child.

In the second stage (July 1998), the basic child benefit and the enriched WIS allotments were combined to form the new CCTB/NCB, which amounts to $1,625 for the first child and $1,425 for each additional child. These CCTB payments are equivalent to the sum of the CTB basic credit and the enriched WIS that took effect in July 1997. The table below shows how this works by comparing the base Child Tax Benefit and the WIS from which the new CCTB/NCB is being developed. It also presents the July 1997 enriched WIS levels, and the value of the 1998 CCTB/NCB.

Why is this new system flawed? Consider the following. First, according to Mr. Martin's 1997–98 budget, the enriched CCTB represents a new financial commitment of $850 million. According to Mr. Martin this comprises $600 million in "new money" starting in July 1998, as well as the $250 million WIS increase announced in the 1996 budget. In addition there is the $850 million allocated in the 1998-99 budget that will be transferred to the provinces and territories in July 1999 and July 2000 payments.

It is a mistake, however, to treat this as new money as was suggested in the 1997-98 budget and implied in the 1998–99 budget address. Rather, it constitutes nothing more than a small repayment of funds that have been siphoned from federal transfer payments to the provinces for social assistance since the introduction of the Canada Health and Social Transfer

Table 1
The Base Child Tax Benefit, The July 1997 Enriched WIS
and the July 1998 Proposed Canada Child
Tax Benefit (CCTB)/National Child Benefit (NCB)

Child Tax Credit Base	Pre-1997 Benefit* with WIS	CTB with 1997 enriched WIS	1998 CCTB/ NCB	Potential Provincial Deduction
1 child	$1,020	$1,520	$1,625	$1,625	$ 605
2 children	$2,040	$2,540	$3,050	$3,050	$1,010
3 children	$3,135	$3,635	$4,475	$4,475	$1,340
4 children	$4,230	$4,730	$5,900	$5,900	$1,670

* Plus $213 for each child under seven when no child care expenses are claimed.

(Source: Canada 1997a, 1997b, and 1997c.)

(CHST) in April 1996. With the elimination of the Canada Assistance Plan (CAP) that cost-shared provincial welfare assistance and services, and the introduction of the CHST, the federal government will have reduced its welfare transfers to provinces by over $7 billion between April 1996 and April 1998. In addition, the dollars allocated for the CCTB/NCB constitute federal transfers that replace money previously paid by provincial and territorial governments to families with children on public assistance. Under the new agreement, provinces and territories will be able to recoup income benefits paid to children on public assistance from the dollars earmarked for children in the CCTB/NCB. When these qualifications are considered it seems clear that little if any new money will be transferred to poor families with children, given that the majority of Canada's poor children live in families on public assistance.

A second problem is that as a benefit directed to poor children, one would expect the announced entitlement increases to be established according to the financial needs of families supporting children. Instead, in Stage 1, they are based on the work status of parents. This is a fundamental flaw. A benefit that is purportedly earmarked for children in poor families should not be contingent on the workforce participation of parents. In practice this means that more than 60 percent of Canada's poor children will gain nothing from this new program (Valpy 1997). What the government has done is bolster the distinction between the "deserving" and "undeserving" poor. This disenfranchising of poor children without parents in the workforce suggests that, in the view of the federal and

106

provincial governments, they are less worthy of financial support.

In this respect Stage 1, which took effect in July 1997, like the WIS component of the CTB, is not a children's benefit. Rather it continues to be a WIS scheme, albeit enriched, for working-poor families with children. On its own a WIS has merit. However, it should not be presented as an enriched child benefit as the work status of parents, rather than the financial needs of children, is the criterion for qualifying.

WIS also entrenches a low-wage strategy in a number of ways. First, it is part of a broader welfare strategy aimed at reducing income assistance benefits while increasing the requirement to work. Second, because of these policies, low wages become more attractive even though remuneration levels are unable to meet basic needs. In this context, WIS makes low-wage jobs more tolerable, enlarging the pool of people willing to take up low-wage jobs and thereby intensifying a downward pressure on wages.

A further point is that the CTB and the enriched WIS are not indexed to inflation. As noted by Campaign 2000 (1997), over time this erodes the value of the benefit for poor families with children while it saves the federal government $160 million annually.

What about Stage 2 that combines the basic CTB with the restructured WIS to form the new CCTB/NCB? While the work status of parents is no longer the standard for receiving extra benefits, income source becomes the yardstick for determining whether families actually will benefit financially from the proposed CCTB/NCB. As clarified in the intergovernmental paper on the NCB, the federal government will permit provinces and territories to deduct a sum equivalent to the enriched WIS component of the CCTB/NCB from income assistance payments made to families with children. This will fortify the distinction between the "deserving" and "undeserving" poor. The "undeserving," as in Stage 1, are poor families with children who rely on public assistance. The "deserving," those who actually benefit financially from the CCTB/NCB, are working-poor families with children who draw no income from provincial income assistance.

The key phrase in the budget documents is that "families on social assistance would receive no less overall" than they currently obtain through provincial and territorial welfare payments (Canada 1997a: 6). This strategy is confirmed in *Working Together Towards a National Child Benefit,* the paper presented by the three levels of government. As federal benefits increase with the new CCTB/NCB in July 1998, "provinces and territories will decrease benefits for social assistance recipients. This decrease will not exceed the amount of the federal increase—the total benefit available to social assistance families will remain at least the same" (Canada 1997b:9). In effect, the provinces and territories are able to deduct a sum that is equal to the enriched WIS component of the CCTB/NCB from welfare payments made to families with children. The potential values of this deduction are $605 for a family with one child and $1,670 for a family with four children (see Table 1).

What this means is that these families will gain nothing financially from the new CCTB/NCB. In effect, the income of these families will remain pegged at the current rates (these are far below accepted standards of income adequacy) in the provinces and territories.

Another key phrase is that "enriched federal benefits will enable provinces and territories to redirect" extra social assistance funds to "other programs targeted at improving work incentives and supporting children in low income families" (Canada 1997a:6; Canada 1997c:19). Again this tactic is confirmed in *Working Together Towards a National Child Benefit* (Canada 1997b), which proposes a reinvestment fund for financing these programs. These reinvestment dollars will come from "funds that provinces/territories would have otherwise spent on social assistance" (Canada 1997b:10). The total value of this reinvestment pool will be equal to the dollar value of the CCTB/NCB deductions taken from welfare payments to families with children.

One further point regarding these proposed services also is warranted. Many of the services to be financed by this reinvestment pool envisioned by the federal, provincial and territorial governments previously were legally mandated through the Canada Assistance Plan. With the CHST, these mandated services were lost. Now it appears that these services and benefits will be financed in part through the monies earmarked for children in poverty. It is clear, however, that most of this money will be used for low-income working families. Current documentation on the CCTB/NCB says very little about services and benefits for families and children whose main source of income is public assistance (Canada 1997a:6). In effect, CAP provisions that disallowed workfare as a condition for receipt of assistance and services now are being replaced by a system of services based on a work-test.

The Saskatchewan Child Benefit: A Case Example

The new Saskatchewan Child Benefit (SCB) is an interesting case example. In some ways, it appears to represent a "best case scenario" of the potential variations that will ensue as provinces merge their programs with that of the federal government beginning July 1, 1998. Families with equivalent numbers of children whose incomes fall below a specified income threshold (or within a specified income range) will receive the same total combined federal and provincial child benefit regardless of income source. This provision departs from the practice in other provinces such as B.C., where the combined federal and provincial child benefit is higher for working-poor families than for those in receipt of income assistance. In Saskatchewan, although it would seem that no distinction is drawn between the working and non-working poor, for reasons detailed below, the intuitive appeal and apparent even-handedness of the SCB in this regard is more apparent than real.

Furthermore, in adopting the rhetoric of the federal government by presenting the SCB as "an investment in children" (Government of Saskatchewan 1998: 9), the Saskatchewan government reinforces the misinformation that all children benefit financially from the new benefit. On the contrary, adhering strictly to the minimum federal government requirement, the new SCB will ensure that families on social assistance will be no better off financially than they were under the previous arrangement.[2] In fact, the provincial contribution to child benefit payments for families on social assistance actually declines under the SCB. While low-income families with children who have a parent in the workforce will receive additional income from the province, this allocation is funded primarily by reducing the province's child benefit payments to families on income assistance.

These points are illustrated below by comparing social assistance and working families with one child and income under $15,921, the income cut-off at which the maximum SCB is paid.

Under the new SCB both of these family types will receive a maximum monthly federal–provincial child benefit of $210. It appears that regardless of the work status of parents, these families will be treated equally. However, the reality is more complex. Because of the average incomes of those in receipt of income assistance compared with the working poor, it is not entirely accurate or fair to treat these groups as having equivalent incomes and therefore as being treated equally by the SCB. Families, in particular single parents, who receive income assistance have incomes that fall much further below the income threshold ($15,921) at which the maximum SCB is paid. For example, in 1995 in Saskatchewan, the maximum income assistance benefit for a single parent family with one child was $10,381 (NCW 1996/97:16). For single parent families with one child, a comparison of the total average income of those who receive and do not receive income assistance reveals a wide disparity: on average, the income of the former group is only 55 percent of the latter (NCW 1996/97:29). Consequently, working-poor families who will be eligible for the SCB are likely to have incomes that lie much closer to, or exceed, the $15,921 income threshold. It is because of the pattern of average incomes of the working poor and those in receipt of income assistance relative to this income threshold that "equal" treatment of families under this particular income level is tantamount to providing a differential income benefit which favours the working poor. Thus, while the SCB appears to meet the policy objective of treating equivalent income groups equally, it is probably more effective as a work incentive initiative.

When looked at in terms of the financial arrangements in place prior to the SCB, it is clear also that the province will cut back its payments to social assistance families, while topping up the federal CCTB/NCB with a provincial supplement for working families of up to $75.

Prior to the introduction of the SCB a family on social assistance with one child receives $160 from the province and $85 from the CCTB. The $160 consists of a $125 Saskatchewan Assistance Plan (SAP) child benefit and $35 from the Saskatchewan Family Income Plan (FIP). This $35 FIP payment, however, is deducted from the CCTB and retained by the Saskatchewan government, reducing this federal benefit to $50. This means that prior to the introduction of the SCB the province actually outlays $125 (not $160) in child benefit payments for social assistance families with one child.

The total federal/provincial child supplement therefore equals $210 per month: $50 from the CCTB, $35 from FIP and $125 through SAP child benefits (see Table 2). In contrast, the poorest of working-poor families (those with incomes less than $10,200 per year) received a maximum FIP payment of $35, a $50 CCTB ($85 minus $35), plus the $50 WIS if their working income fell between $10,000 and $20,921 annually. This means that the maximum combined provincial/federal payments for these working-poor families amounted to $135 per month.

Under the SCB one-child families (social assistance and families in paid employment) with incomes under $15,921 will both receive $210 per month in combined federal/provincial child benefits. For families on social assistance this child supplement is divided into the following sources under the SCB: $85 from the CCTB, $50 from the NCB (Government of Saskatchewan 1998:9) and now only a $75 provincial top-up (previously provided through SAP). In effect the Saskatchewan government's payment to social assistance families with one child will be reduced by $50 per month (from $125 to $75), an amount equal to the federal NCB—or the WIS payments in Stage 1 of the CCTB. Annually the province's financial contribution to child benefits for a family with one child on income assistance will be lowered by $605, which is equal to the potential provincial deduction in social assistance payments noted in Table 1.

For families with a parent in paid employment and income under $15,921, the $210 SCB consists of $135 in federal money (the $85 CCTB and $50 NCB) and a $75 provincial top-up. Two-thirds of this provincial top-up for working-poor families with one child ($50/$75) is funded from provincial child benefits previously paid to income assistance recipients through SAP. In the end, income assistance recipients are no worse-off because the enhanced federal contribution through the NCB is equal to this provincial deduction. Nevertheless, most of the Saskatchewan portion of

Table 2

The Saskatchewan Child Benefit (SCB) for Income Assistance and "Working" Poor Families Prior to and After the Introduction of the SCB[1]

Income Assistance Families				Working-Poor Families			
Prior to the SCB		The SCB (July 1998)		Prior to the SCB		The SCB (July 1998)	
SAP	$160 $125 SAP Child Benefit* $ 35 FIP Payment*	SCB	$ 75	FIP	$ 35	SCB	$ 75
CCTB	$ 85 (-$35 FIP Payment)*	CCTB	$ 85	CCTB	$ 50 ($85-$35)	CCTB	$ 85
Actual CCTB	$ 50	NCB	$ 50	WIS	$ 50	NCB	$ 50
Total	$210	Total	$210	Total	$135	Total	$210

1. Calculations based on a family with one child and incomes < or = to $15, 921.
* Plus $213 for each child under seven when no child care expenses are claimed.

the new integrated SCB for the working poor is funded by a horizontal transfer of provincial funds from the poorest of the poor (social assistance families) to working-poor families.

Although there is no new provincial money for income assistance recipients, there appears to be $25 per month in new provincial money in the SCB for this family type. Even so, the threshold for receiving the top-up is so low that many working-poor families with one child will not receive the full SCB entitlement. If the basic CCTB threshold ($25,921) was used instead, many more families with children would be helped financially and the likelihood of a reduction in child poverty would be more realistic.

Regarding the goal of poverty reduction the SCB fails in two ways. First, because the SCB does not increase the incomes of social assistance families (the poorest of the poor), its "investment in children" excludes the majority of poor children. Second, the SCB limits assistance to many working-poor families, as the value of the SCB begins to decline at a very low income threshold.

111

Conclusion

The rhetoric accompanying the CCTB/NCB portrays it as an investment in children that is designed to reduce child poverty. In practice the reduction of child poverty is clearly a secondary objective. The major impetus behind this new system of child benefits is to move people from welfare into work by providing financial incentives that ensure that the incomes of working-poor families with children are higher than families on income assistance (Canada 1997b). The additional CCTB/NCB income in Stage 2 (as is the case in Stage 1) is no more than a working income supplement geared to assist the transition from welfare into the workforce for families with children. At one level this may be a worthy purpose. It helps to reduce the welfare wall where moving into work involves added work-related expenses, such as lower employment incomes compared with what one receives from welfare, and a loss of in-kind benefits that are available to income assistance beneficiaries. According to the Caledon Institute of Social Policy (Battle and Mendelson 1997:3) the "promotion of labour force attachment" is a "reasonable objective" of the CCTB/NCB. Caledon argues that the WIS-equivalent supplement "encourages parents to risk leaving welfare" and to "remain in the workforce" once they have returned to work. There is some value in supplementing the incomes of people who have moved into paid employment from welfare. However, it needs to be stressed that the CCTB/NCB is packaged as a child benefit, not a work supplement. What we have instead is a work supplement where the needs of children appear to be incidental. The evidence to support this assertion is that the majority of Canada's poor children are disqualified from these additional CCTB/NCB income benefits because they come from families who receive income assistance (either because they are not in the workforce, or because they earn minimum wages at a part-time job).

This supplement perhaps would be more palatable if it was presented for what it is—a WIS that is designed to move families with children from welfare to work. But even this objective is questionable. The CCTB/NCB is being implemented during a time of high and persistent unemployment. The structure of opportunity is collapsing. Finding paid employment to get off welfare is not an easy task when jobs are not available. This key issue is not fully acknowledged in this piece of neo-liberal social policy. Nor is there adequate recognition of other legitimate factors (child-rearing responsibilities, inadequate day care, sickness etc.) that explain the need for parental reliance on income assistance. For example, caring for children (the reason many single parents are on income assistance) is in itself a significant contribution that is undervalued. The CCTB/NCB clearly discriminates against single parents who have no way of supporting themselves while caring for their children full or part time. Despite this, the government has chosen to pursue a policy that suggests that parents and children from working-poor families (Stage 1), whose main source of income comes from employment (Stage 2), are more deserving of assistance than children raised in families that receive provincial income assistance. As a result these families and children, the poorest of the poor, are screened out of this new system of child benefits.

The 1998 federal budget announcement of a further $850 million to be allocated to the CCTB/NCB brings to the fore more unanswered questions and concerns. One of the purported strengths of the CCTB/NCB is that as it matures it will combine "the dollars currently spent on social assistance [for children]," federal child expenditures and "other family supports" into a single, integrated child benefit for low-income families with children (CCSD 1997a:1; Battle and Mendelsohn 1997). The reality, however, is that as this benefit matures (as witnessed in Stage 2 that began in July 1998), it continues to be bifurcated. This bifurcation occurs because of the differentiation of an equivalent-to-the-WIS component of the CCTB/NCB for income assistance recipients, as provinces are allowed to deduct an equivalent sum from provincial payments to children in families who receive income assistance. For the time being, then, the benefit is structured so that income assistance recipients with children will be no worse-off than they are under provincial income assistance programs. This conservative objective effectively exonerates legislated poverty by pegging combined federal/provincial child benefit contribution levels for income assistance recipients to the status quo. But will this rather minimal degree of protection be maintained in the future? What will happen over time? Will the value of the WIS component deducted from income assistance by the provinces/territories remain at its present level or will it increase and if so, on what basis? Given the structure of the program, it would be in the financial and political interests of the provinces and territories to see the value of the WIS-equivalent component rise, as this will lead to reductions in provincial/territorial expenditures earmarked for social assistance. But on what basis would this increase take place: inflation, in step with increases in the value of the overall benefit, or according to rises in income assistance rates in a particular province/territory? The answers to these questions are important in terms of the future financial status of families with children in receipt of income assistance and the CCTB/NCB. Although the federal government has not yet announced the details of the proposed two-phase increase in the CCTB/NCB, its structure has considerable implications for the financial well-being of families on income assistance.

Social policy involves making choices. In considering new legislation it is important to ask who wins, who loses, and what role does the state play in reducing or reinforcing existing income and other forms of inequalities. In terms of the new Canada Child Tax Benefit/National Child Benefit the answers to these questions are quite clear. At one level working-poor families with children gain something, although only a rather paltry sum. As noted by the Vanier Institute of the Family, the new supplement to the working poor, on average, amounts to $2.13 a day. The federal government may be the biggest winner as it appears to be doing something about children in poverty. However close scrutiny of the new benefit system shows that there is really no new money, and that additional cash components will not go to the poorest of poor children. The provinces and territories are also winners as part of the money they previously spent on social assistance for families with children can be recouped, and replaced with the CCTB/NCB benefit.

The real losers are families, including their children, who rely primarily on welfare. Recent estimates show that there are some 1,472,000 poor children, in 771,000 families (Campaign 2000 1997). There is no extra cash for approximately 60 percent of these families and their children because they rely on public assistance. In this respect, the new CCTB/NCB ends up reinforcing the impoverishment of the poorest of poor children in this country. What the federal Liberals, as well as the provinces and territories, are doing is cementing a neo-liberal agenda where the benevolence and concern for Canada's poorest children is more apparent than real.

Notes

1. For example, British Columbia, Saskatchewan, Yukon, Prince Edward Island, Newfoundland and Labrador, and Alberta either have or are instituting health plans for low income families that will allow them to leave social assistance without losing these benefits.
2. Newfoundland appears to be the only province which is passing on to income assistance recipients the full value of the NCB supplement.

6

So There You Go!

Pete Hudson

Introduction

A graduate student, bright enough to get away with it, once wrote as a conclusion to a term paper, "so there you go!" In the case of the National Child Benefit (NCB), however, some attempt at a less cryptic closure is probably necessary. This does not mean declaring a winner in the debate, rather the need to reflect on it and pose some of the questions that need to be addressed as social policy analysts and anti-poverty activists go forward. As a starting point I examine the areas of agreement and disagreement before moving on to suggest the basis for evaluating the NCB over the next five to ten years. I end with some comments on the broader context of the NCB and its implications for anti-poverty policy.

The Areas of Agreement

Here are two sets of authors, all experienced social policy analysts, all of whom enjoy reputations as progressive people, apparently disagreeing quite sharply on the merits of the first anti-poverty measure to come from the federal government in thirty years. Yet there are large areas of agreement. The first of these is that the NCB is not even a partial anti-poverty measure: it is, even on its own merits, only a first step to a partial response. Even its proponents acknowledge that the program so far is more potential than actual. The overall amounts allocated to the program are relatively small, the net benefits to each beneficiary are commensurably small and a large number of potential beneficiaries are excluded from receiving any direct benefits (mainly those whose primary source of income is provincial social assistance). All seem to agree that for the NCB to achieve its own modest promise as an anti-poverty measure, these flaws must be attended to. Ken Battle, for example, proposes specific figures for an adequate level of child benefits very close to those proposed by Campaign 2000 (Novick and Shillington 1997).

Second, all the contributors are agreed that even if the program maximizes its promise in the near future, far more than income support to low-income families is required for poverty in Canada to be significantly alleviated. Other initiatives must include full employment policies, minimum wage and other regulatory measures for the workforce, the encouragement as opposed to the disparagement of a healthy collective bargaining process, a fairer tax system, social housing, expanded day care, maintenance and improvement of universal health care, education, personal social services and inexpensive, effective public transportation.

Third, all the contributors are agreed that of the two major objectives stated for the program—alleviation of child poverty and providing work incentives—the latter is at least as prominent as the former. This is less obvious in the way the federal government has represented the program (that is, as an anti-child poverty measure) but more obvious in the provisions of the program.

Finally, all are agreed that some poor people will be marginally better off under the NCB than they were before it. There is also agreement on some specific flaws in the program: the current inadequacy of benefits and the need for its extension to all low-income families. The proponents of the program recognize its current flaws, and the critics recognize some immediate merit.

The Areas of Disagreement

While there are disagreements about the actual level of benefits—which groups will benefit the most and when, how many families will be excluded (depending on what portions of the poor are waged and non-waged)—that is, about the rules and mechanics of the program, critics most often disagree with what they see as the underlying ideology and politics of the NCB.

The proponents base their case on the relationship between those whose source of income is the paid labour market and those whose source is social assistance. Their argument cannot be solely dismissed as the old chestnut of "less eligibility." There is a case to made that the working poor ought to receive more benefits than they now do. Moreover, to the extent that the NCB eases the transition for parents receiving social assistance to move into the paid labour force, so much the better. Furthermore, they argue that, paradoxically, over time the new system will break down the distinctions between the groups.

The ground argued by the program's critics is quite different: namely that the program may be *inherently* flawed because certainly in effect, and likely in intent, it promotes a system of rewards based on relationships to the labour force. The critics argue that this orientation fails to recognize the labour of caregiving and the value that ought to be placed on work that is currently unpaid (or in the case of social allowances paid at rates approaching 50 percent below the poverty line). The "welfare wall," which both sides understand to exist, is not the difference between benefits available to the working poor and the non-working poor. It is the difference between those whose work is *visible* as waged labour and those whose labour is *invisible* as non-waged labour. This last point (more than incidentally) illustrates some major differences in the kind of language used by the contenders in the debate. Another example is the use by Ken Battle of words like "staggering" to describe the cost, estimated at $15 billion, required to eliminate child poverty. Such language is avoided by critics of the scheme who might use the same word to describe foregone revenues in such schemes as the special tax treatment accorded retirement savings, which in 1993 cost the treasury $16 billion (CCPA and Cho!ces, 1998).[1]

Often this disagreement about whether or not the NCB is *inherently* flawed is more implicit than explicit. Proponents argue that the flaws are remediable with time and commitment. In this view, the basic framework for a sound program is in place, and maximum impact is potentially realizable as dollars are added in future years. On the other side, it is not clear if the critics are suggesting that the NCB should be scrapped entirely, in part because specific alternatives are not articulated by them. It appears the critics are saying that the program *by its very nature* does more harm than good. In the work-incentive feature of the program, for example, the critics imply that it unavoidably damages the interests, self esteem and community regard of those not in the wage-labour market. What should follow is a call to return the NCB to the drawing board, but this is only implied by its critics. The debate does not move to consider possible remedies, such as governments assisting this group to tell their stories and reversing the poor-bashing (illustrated not just in benefit cuts but in the use of pejorative language in characterizing this population) in which many have so shamefully indulged in the past decade. In other words, there is a piece missing from the debate which still leaves open the question of whether the NCB is a non-starter or if it is rescuable.

The final point of disagreement seems to be around the values of the NCB and the importance attached to the work-incentive goal as opposed to the alleviation of child poverty. There are three possible constructions on this issue. One is that a work-incentive feature is not only acceptable, but actually redresses some historical unfairness on the anti-poverty front. The second is that the work-incentive feature is nothing more than one more service to international capital among many other recent government moves to show Canada as "open for business." A third construction says of course the NCB serves international capital, as the same could be said of most of our postwar social programs: social allowances and the former unemployment insurance program maintained a reserve labour force. Worker's compensation provides a cheap insurance program for capital. Doug Durst's introductory chapter documents the appeal of the former family allowance program as a strategy for dampening expected postwar wage demands. Recent erosion of social programs is explained by that same persistent and sometimes perverse relationship between social and economic policy (business decided that these programs no longer serve its best interests). Thus debate around the merits of a particular program might, at every opportunity, point to this relationship between the power of capital and social policy development, but at the same time ask who else is benefiting. In other words does some significant and needy subgroup of the public enterprise benefit, or only the shareholders of the private enterprise? In the struggle, what gains were made and what was given by those advocating stronger social programs?

Evaluating the NCB

Whether we praise or condemn it, the NCB is now with us. In monitoring its effects, and seeking to ensure that it maximizes whatever potential it may have as an anti-poverty strategy, what are social policy analysts looking for? Ken Battle and Karen Swift and Mike Birmingham have proposed criteria to evaluate the program: the former focusing on the NCB, with the latter proposing more general criteria against which to judge any social-policy measure (illustrative again of the different ground from which each present their earlier case). These proposals speak for themselves, and the only comment worth making at this stage is that these two sorts of criteria seem more complimentary than contradictory. Most particularly, in relation to the specifics of the NCB, the timeliness of benefit payments, their application regardless of source of income and their adequacy (including full indexing) require evaluation. A few additions are offered here, also focused in the more narrow sense on the NCB.

First, the program has been structured around the results of federal–provincial negotiations, whereby the savings to the provinces, enabled through funds provided by the federal government to social assistance recipients, must be spent on other anti-poverty programs. These latter programs must be subject to scrutiny. So far these programs are mostly "blank cheques" and yet they are a critical and substantial part of the NCB. We must ensure that they specify who is to benefit, how they are expected to benefit and the relationship between the ends and the means (not a strong point of many provincial programs). There is a particular need to see if they offer anything to the unwaged labourer/caregiver. Furthermore, the argument that a sufficiency of cash income is a prerequisite to well-being but not a guarantee of it needs to be expanded and explained. What sorts of programs in this context might compensate in part for shortfalls of cash income? There would seem, for example, to be an essential difference between funds dedicated to teaching people to budget income which the teachers themselves could not live on, and the dedication of those funds to, say, social housing.[2] A nutrition program might mean a regular hot meal for a child who otherwise would not receive it, or it might mean distributing the Canada Food Guide to mothers who have no money and no transportation. Above all, the use by the provinces of the savings to increase cash or other direct benefits to adults on social assistance, the separation of whose well-being from that of their children is a particularly troubling feature of the NCB, could be a significant anti-poverty measure. In short, the program should be understood and evaluated not just on the basis of the CCTC provisions alone, but also on how the role assigned to the provinces as part of the larger NCB is played out and how the two components mesh.[3]

Second, since it is acknowledged as a major objective, the work-incentive aspect of the program must be closely monitored. Not only the numbers of those enabled to enter the workforce through the incentive, but more importantly the quality of the outcomes for those who do so require scrutiny. Are such jobs marginal and, even with what is, in effect, a wage subsidy, still barely subsistence? Are they temporary—as has been the fate of many workfare programs—with those who have been given hope of struggling their way out of the poverty of welfare via paid employment back on the rolls a short time later in greater despair than ever before?

Particularly important to monitor is the relationship between income support programs and wages. Higher levels of social assistance have been hypothesized to exert upward pressure on minimum wages. Has the erosion of rates through lack of indexing and specific cuts had a downward pressure on wages?[4] Might an overall increase in social assistance rates through whatever means (federal or provincial benefits) exert some upward pressure on wages? An increase in social assistance rates might discourage entry into paid employment, because the welfare wall is restored, but both the waged worker and the non-waged worker would be better off. In relation to the CCTC in particular, will the wage subsidy feature act to permanently depress wages at the lower end, and if so, is that remediable (as, for example, in higher minimum-wage requirements)?

Beyond the NCB

The common agreement that alleviating poverty requires multiple, intersecting policies, not just income supports—even there not just by means of a single tax credit program—has been mentioned earlier in this chapter and in preceding chapters. A detailed discussion of such policies is beyond the scope of this book (but is taken up by others—see Novick and

Stillington, 1988; CCPA/Cho!ces 1997 and 1998; and Cohen 1997). However, there are some general comments which are germane to the more specific debate about the NCB.

The first observes that much of the debate on the NCB centres around the issues of fairness of treatment between two already marginalized groups. Thus as the past record of providing few benefits to one group (the waged poor) is partially redressed in the new program, the issue of fairness to a now relatively more disadvantaged group (the non-waged group) surfaces. A part of the debate revolves around the lost in-kind benefits as the non-waged poor try to move into the ranks of the waged poor. Is it being too simplistic to suggest that were such benefits available on a universal basis (or at least on the same basis as the cash benefits), that much of the debate around the welfare wall would be redundant? Had anti-poverty advocates been successful in negotiating some expansion of benefits such as dental and eye care, health and drug plans, employment insurance, social housing, public transportation, accessible recreational opportunities and the like, instead of having to watch successive governments at all levels roll back such benefits and opportunities, the trade-offs between wage and non-wage labour would virtually disappear. If the doctrine of "less eligibility" for the non-waged poor must persist into yet another century, its impact is much modified if these major quality of life components are available to this group on the same basis as for the rest of the population—independent of the size and source of income.

Secondly, it seems that we need to campaign for a *culture shift*. It should have two faces. One is to press for a culture shift in which Canadians recognize certain levels of income supports but also other contributions to health and well-being as *entitlements*. T.H. Marshall called these social rights.[5] A belief in the right of all citizens to an array of services and supports has never been achieved in Canada. We are presently witnessing a retreat from this view, when we need instead a renewed commitment to it. Thus, one of the problematic aspects of the NCB, for example, is its discretionary character. There are no guarantees that funds will be added to the CCTC in subsequent years even though they have been promised, or that the provinces will deliver on their part in the NCB.

This is a sad irony. In the introductory chapter, Doug Durst discusses the U.N. Convention on the Rights of the Child, which endorses Marshall's concept of social rights. It makes specific reference to many social rights, including social security and income supports for children and their caregivers (Articles 26 & 27). The convention, to which Canada is a signatory, is not about discretionary benefits. It is about entitlements. The strongest way to ensure social rights is to reference them in the Constitution, and if that is an impossible dream, it is at least an ideal to aim for.[6] In any event, perhaps the most important gain to be measured is the degree of public acceptance of the entitlement principle rather than the ways in which it is enshrined.

The other face of the culture shift concerns the ways Canadians think about taxation. This is not a reference to the need for a more progressive system, which is largely accepted by most anti-poverty advocates. Rather I am referring to the (widely accepted) contention that citizens are all overtaxed, that taxes are bad (as in the phrase "tax burden") and that in an ideal world, nobody would pay any taxes. Canadians would just buy what they need in a marketplace laden with all the goodies they could possibly need or want.

The taxes-are-bad argument sidesteps not just the issue of who pays or does not pay taxes, but also fails to acknowledge that taxes are, on a more fundamental level, simply another way of purchasing goods and services. Many of these, such as clean air or safe workplaces, are not available in other ways. Most others, such as health care, or physical infrastructure are not available as effectively or efficiently. The difference between de-insuring prescription drugs and insuring them, for example, is that in the former case the sick pay directly, while in the latter the risk is spread over the whole population. One way or the other Canadians still pay. In short, much of what Canadians value in their quality of life has been supplied (income assistance), contracted (hospitals) or regulated (food protection) by our governments from the collective pot. The only relevant question to put to any given government is whether taxes are value for money, not how much we are paying in absolute taxes. The "tax burden" phraseology is just another marketing strategy to justify the ideology of a residual state. We must deal with the fact that there is lots of work to be done but few (paid) jobs by redeploying more resources into caring for the sick, the old, children, the distressed, the overburdened and mother earth. For this to happen the role of taxation has to be reframed, because it is the only vehicle through which, to my (perhaps limited) imagination, such caring work can be achieved.[7] Governments will have to be willing to capture the fruits of productivity gains and be supported by the populace in doing so.

Finally, none of the above is likely to occur unless Canadians can re-enlist our governments in the service of the citizenry instead of international capital, and stand with them in weaning themselves away from the dangers of capital dependency—ever present but sharply increased in recent years. Social as well as economic well-being is now represented as synonymous with competing to attract international capital in the race to the bottom. That race leads to low wages, a docile workforce, externalities absorbed by the environment and our health and foregone revenues that could pay for caring work and the new NCB (which, without detracting from its progressive potential, is as much a work incentive and a subsidy to capital as it is an anti-poverty measure). Much of the struggle for progressive social policy, including anti-poverty strategies, will revolve around working to divert resources currently dedicated to this race to the bottom into a revival of the co-operative movement, support for micro enterprises, public and quasi-public services and any other social and economic enterprise that does not hold our well-being to ransom with the threat of capital flight.

Thus, understanding our dependency on business helps in understanding the NCB and the context within which it has emerged. Higher levels of unemployment mean higher take-up rates of social allowances. The experience of the past two decades indicates that the business community cannot be counted on to reduce unemployment. At best this goal is incidental to its interests; at worst it benefits from high rates of unemployment. This leaves the creation of some sizeable portion of jobs to the public and quasi-public sector. Insofar as job creation can occur outside the marketplace, the pool of non-waged poor becomes smaller, which should lead to a lessening of the obsession with further diminishing the pool that characterizes some aspects of the NCB. Total dependency on international capital to create jobs places citizens and their governments at its mercy. Whenever social policy issues bump up against its interests (which in the case of income supports is frequently), business will continue to influence and perhaps distort the goals of social programs, and even ensure starvation of resources to them.

Perhaps we can agree that the NCB has some progressive features. Certainly the notion of an income-tested program and a tax credit formula has received some broad acceptance.[8] Furthermore, it does have the potential to be more than it is now. Close scrutiny as it unfolds over the next decade is clearly necessary to see if that potential is achieved.

The image of the phoenix is one far too dramatic to apply to the NCB. It implies something fully fledged and fully functioning—an instant rebirth. On the other hand, a fizzle implies something with a brief life span quickly followed by demise. The NCB may have quite a long life, although how useful to the 1.5 million Canadian children now in poverty remains to be seen. If the imagery is to be pursued, I prefer to understand the NCB as a green log tossed into the remaining embers of our social programs. On the understanding that one program can achieve only so much in the war on poverty, the task now becomes to add the extra fuel alongside the NCB and fan the embers. In this regard I am reminded of a passionately delivered sentence from an anti-poverty activist at the microphone of a public meeting held last year: "I'm in for the long haul."

Notes

1. Also CBC Radio National News, on the morning of September 21, 1998, reported a projected surplus in the federal budget for the current fiscal year in excess of $10 billion—over two-thirds of the $15 billion required to eliminate child poverty.

2. Any one of a host of examples could have been used here. Social housing is particularly relevant since according to the National Council of Welfare only 8 percent of all families receiving social allowances were in subsidized housing of any kind (NCW 1998c). The virtual halt of social housing provisions by all three levels of government has been particularly harsh for social allowance recipients. The relationship between the well-being of children, their families and their communities, and stable, affordable housing has been documented in many places (see for example, Novick and Shillington 1997 or Cohen 1997).

3. This is not to say that I am sanguine about the provinces taking on the role of champions of the poor. The comment about their role, as with much of the rest of the commentary in this chapter, addresses the question of what the social policy community might want to see happen, rather than what might be politically feasible.

4. We do know that there has been a decline in real wages over the last ten years at the lower end of the wage scale. We cannot say for sure the extent, if any, to which this can be attributed to declining social allowance rates. It will be difficult to isolate this factor from others such as the replacement of production jobs with service jobs, neglect of minimum wage legislation, weakening of collective bargaining and so forth.

5. T.H. Marshall was a major social policy analyst during the period of growth in the welfare state in Britain in the postwar period. He understood citizenship in the fullest sense of that word as being composed of civil rights, political rights and social rights. The last were the most important not just for their own sake, but because the exercise of the other two was dependent for most citizens on the continuous expansion of social rights (Marshall 1965 and 1975).

6. The next best thing is in legislation even though the lack of enforcement of the adequacy provisions of the Canada Assistance Plan illustrate its shortcomings. Its abolition represented a loss in the principle, but materially not much.

7. This does not speak to the debate about an expanded role for the third sector in caring work. Whether the state delivers services directly or whether it chooses to support the third sector to carry on some portion of this work, the issue of the source of funds remains. The third sector cannot sustain this work without substantial support from tax revenues.

8. The last two Federal Alternative Budgets for example, which received input from hundreds of grassroots meetings across the country, proposed tax credits as one anti-poverty strategy.

Bibliography

Armitage, A. 1996. *Social Welfare in Canada Revisited*. Don Mills, ON: Oxford University Press.

Baines, C., P. Evans and S. Neysmith. 1991. *Women's Caring: A Feminist Perspective on Social Welfare*. Toronto: McClelland and Stewart.

Baker, M. 1998. *Poverty, Social Assistance and the Employability of Low-Income Mothers: Cross-National Comparisons*. Ottawa: Human Resources.

Battle, Ken. 1997. *Persistent Poverty*. Ottawa: Caledon Institute of Social Policy.

———. (Under the pseudonym Gratton Gray). 1990. "Social Policy by Stealth." *Policy Options* 11, 2 (March).

Battle, Ken, and Michael Mendelson. 1997. *Child Benefit Reform in Canada: An Evaluative Framework and Future Directions*. Ottawa: Caledon Institute of Social Policy.

Battle, Ken, and Leon Muszynski. 1995. *One Way to Fight Child Poverty*. Ottawa: Caledon Institute of Social Policy.

Battle, Ken, and Sherri Torjman. 1993. *The Welfare Wall: The Interaction of the Welfare and Tax Systems*. Ottawa: Caledon Institute of Social Policy.

Burman, P. 1996. *Poverty's Bonds, Power and Agency in the Social Relations of Welfare*. Toronto: Thompson Educational Publishing.

Caledon Institute of Social Policy. 1997. *The Down Payment Budget*. Ottawa: Caledon Institute of Social Policy.

Campaign 2000. 1997. *Child Poverty in Canada: Report Card 1996*. Toronto: Campaign 2000.

Canada. 1998a. *Poverty Profile 1996*. A Report by the National Council of Welfare. ncw@magi.com. Ottawa: Minister of Public Works and Government Services.

———. 1998b. Statistics Canada. Internet: www.statcan.ca

———. 1998c. *Income Distribution by Size in Canada, 1996*. Ottawa: Statistics Canada.

———. 1997a. *Towards a National Child Benefit System*. Ottawa: Department of Finance.

———. 1997b. *Working Together Towards A National Child Benefit*. Ottawa: Department of Finance.

———. 1997c. *The National Child Benefit: Building a Better Future for Canadian Children*. Ottawa: Federal/Provincial/Territorial Ministers Responsible for Social Services.

———. 1991. Convention on the Rights of the Child. Ottawa: Human Rights Directorate.

———. 1989. Commons Debate. November 24:6173–6228. Ottawa: House of Commons.

Canadian Centre for Policy Alternatives & Cho!ces Coalition for Social Justice. 1998. *Alternative Federal Budget Papers 1998*. Halifax: Formac Distributing.

———. 1997. *Alternative Federal Budget Papers 1997*. Halifax: Formac Distributing.

Canadian Council on Children and Youth (CCCY). 1978. *Admittance Restricted, The Child as Citizen in Canada.* Ottawa: Canadian Task Force on the Child as Citizen.

Canadian Council on Social Development (CCSD). 1997a. "Integrating children's benefits: what will result?" Ottawa: Canadian Council on Social Development.

———. 1997b. "CCSD's Response to the 1997 Federal Budget." Ottawa: Canadian Council on Social Development.

———. 1997c. *The Progress of Canada's Children 1997.* Ottawa: Canadian Council on Social Development. Internet: www.ccsd.ca; Email: council@ccsd.ca

Clarke, T. 1998. "The MAI Threat to Canada's Social Programs." *Canadian Review of Social Policy* 41(Spring).

Cohen, Joy. 1997. *Sounding the Alarm: Poverty in Canada.* Ottawa: Queen's Printer.

Collins, Stephanie Baker. 1997. "Child poverty and the federal budget: Is this the best we could do?" *The Catalyst* 20, 1.

Conway, J. 1997. *The Canadian Family in Crisis.* Third Edition. Toronto: James Lorimer & Company.

Davis, L., and J. Hagen. 1996. "Stereotypes and Stigma: What's Changed for Welfare Mothers." *Affilia* 11, 3.

Department of Finance Canada. 1997. *Working Together Towards a National Child Benefit System.* Ottawa: Department of Finance.

Doyal, L., and I. Gough. 1991. *A Theory of Need.* London: Macmillan.

Ellwood, D.T. 1988. *Poor Support.* New York: Basic Books.

Federal and provincial/territorial governments. 1998. *Update on Reinvestments Under the National Child Benefit.* Internet: http://www.intergov.gc.ca/docs/intergov/ncb/ncbpamp-3.htm

———. 1997. *The National Child Benefit: Building a Better Future for Canadian Children.* Internet: http://www.intergov.gc.ca/docs/intergov/ncb/ncbpamp-3.htm

Fisher, B., and J. Tronto. 1990. "Toward a Feminist Theory of Caring." In E.K. Abel and M.D. Nelson (eds.), *Circles of Care: Work and Identity in Women's Lives.* Albany: State University of New York Press.

Fraser, N. 1989. *Unruly Practices: Power, Discourse and Gender in Contemporary Social Theory.* Minneapolis: University of Minnesota Press.

Freiler, C. 1997. "A National Child Benefit: Promising First Step or Final Gesture in Child Poverty Strategy?" *Perspectives on a National Agenda for Canada's Children* 1 (August).

Freiler, C., and J. Cerny. 1998. *Benefiting Canada's Children: Perspectives on Gender and Social Responsibility.* Ottawa: Status of Women Canada. Internet: www.swc-cfc.gc.ca/.; Email: research@swc-cfc.gc.ca

Geller, G., J. Joel and S. Moryski. 1993. *State of Regina's Children: A Statistical Profile.* Regina: Social Administration Research Unit, University of Regina.

Gingrich, N. 1995. *To Renew America.* New York: Harper/Collins.

Government of Saskatchewan. 1998. *Building Independence: Investing in Families.* Regina: Ministry of Social Services.

Graham, H. 1983. "Caring: A Labour of Love." In J. Finch and D. Groves (eds.),

A Labour of Love: Women, Work and Caring. London: Routledge and Kegan Paul.

Guest, D. 1980. *The Emergence of Social Security in Canada*. Vancouver: University of British Columbia Press.

Hawken, P. 1997. "Natural Capitalism." *Mother Jones* March/April.

Hay, D. 1997. "Campaign 2000. Family and Child Poverty in Canada." In J. Pulkingham and G. Ternowetsky (eds.), *Child and Family Policies: Struggles, Strategies and Options*. Halifax: Fernwood Publishing.

Heller, A. 1976. *The Theory of Need in Marx*. New York: St. Martin's Press.

Human Resources Development Canada (HRDC). 1994. *Social Security in Canada*. Ottawa: HRDC.

Hunsley, T. 1996. *Incomes and Outcomes: Lone Parents and Social Policy in Ten Countries*. Kingston, ON: Queen's University School of Policy Studies.

Ignatieff, M. 1984. *The Needs of Strangers*. London: The Hogarth Press.

Kadushin, K., and J.A. Martin. 1988. *Child Welfare Services*. 4th Edition. New York: Macmillan.

Kahnawake Shakotiia'Takehnhas Community Services (KSCS). 1994. *Aboriginal Values and Social Services: The Kahnawake Experience*. Ottawa: Canadian Council on Social Development.

Kitchen, B. 1987. "The Introduction of Family Allowances in Canada." In A. Moscovitch and J. Albert (eds.), *The Benevolent State. The Growth of Welfare in Canada*. Toronto: Garamond Press.

Kitchen, B., and R. Popham. 1998. "The Attack on Motherwork in Ontario." In L. Ricciutelli, J. Larkin and E. O'Neill (eds.), *Confronting the Cuts*. Toronto: Inanna Publications.

Korten, D. 1995. *When Corporations Rule the World*. West Hartford, Conn.: Kumarian Press.

Liberal Party of Canada. 1997. *Securing our Future Together*. Ottawa: Liberal Party of Canada.

Liera, A. 1994. "Concepts of Caring: Loving, Thinking, and Doing." *Social Service Review* 68, 2.

Lindsey, D. 1994. *The Welfare of Children*. New York: Oxford.

Marshall, T. H. 1975. *Social Policy*. London: Hutchinson.

———. 1965. *Class, Citizenship and Social Development*. New York: Doubleday.

McGilly, F. 1998. *An Introduction to Canada's Public Social Services: Understanding Income and Health Programs*. 2nd Edition. Toronto: Oxford University Press.

———. 1990. *An Introduction to Canada's Public Social Services: Understanding Income and Health Programs*. Toronto: McClellland and Stewart Inc.

Mendelson, Michael. 1997. *A Preliminary Analysis of the Impact of the BC Family Bonus on Poverty and on Welfare Caseloads*. Toronto: KPMG.

National Anti-Poverty Organization (NAPO). 1998. *NAPO News*. April, 64.

———. 1997. "Martin Does Nothing to Address 'Third World Poverty'" in Canada." Ottawa: National Anti-Poverty Organization.

National Council of Welfare (NCW). 1998a. *Notes for a Presentation to the Standing Committee on Finance*. Ottawa: National Council of Welfare.

———. 1998b. *Poverty Profile 1996. A Report by the National Council of Welfare*. Ottawa: Minister of Public Works and Government Services Canada.

———. 1998. *Profiles of Welfare: Myths and Realities*. Ottawa: National Council of Welfare.

———. 1997. *Child Benefits: A Small Step Forward*. Ottawa: Minister of Supply and Services Canada.

———. 1996/97. *Welfare Incomes 1995*. Ottawa: Minister of Supply and Services.

———. 1975. *Poor Kids: A Report on Children in Poverty in Canada*. Ottawa: National Council of Welfare.

Noddings, N. 1984. *Caring: A Feminine Approach to Ethics*. Berkeley: University of California Press.

Novick, Marvyn, and Richard Shillington. 1997. *Mission for the Millennium: A Comprehensive Strategy for Children and Youth*. Campaign 2000 Discussion Paper No. 2.

O'Neill, E. 1998. "From Global Economies to Local Cuts: Globalization and Structural Change in Our Own Backyard." In L. Ricciutelli, J. Larkin and E. O'Neill (eds.), *Confronting the Cuts*. Toronto: Inanna Publications.

Ontario Coalition for Better Child Care. 1997. "Ottawa fiddles with child poverty as social programs burn." Toronto: Ontario Coalition for Better Child Care.

Oppenheim, C., and L. Harker. 1996. *Poverty, the Facts*. 3rd Edition. London: Child Poverty Action Group.

Ozawa, M. 1994. "Women, Children, and Welfare Reform. *Affilia* 9, 4.

Pascal, G. 1993. "Citizenship—A Feminist Analysis." In G. Drover and P. Kerans (eds.), *Welfare Theory*. Aldershoot, Eng.: Edward Elgar Publishing.

Pulkingham, Jane, and Gordon Ternowetsky (eds.). 1997. *Child and Family Policies: Struggles, Strategies and Options*. Halifax: Fernwood Publishing.

Pulkingham, Jane, Gordon Ternowetsky and David Hay. 1997. "The New Canada Child Tax Benefit: Eradicating Poverty or Victimizing the Poorest?" *CCPA Monitor* 4, 1.

Rank, M.R. 1994. *Living on the Edge: The Realities of Welfare in America*. New York: Columbia University Press.

Richards, J. 1998. *Retooling the Welfare State: What's to Be Done*. Policy Study 31. Toronto: C.D. Howe Institute.

Rifkin, J. 1995. *The End of Work*. New York: Putnam.

Ross, D.P., E.R. Shillington and C. Lochhead. 1994. *The Canadian Fact Book on Poverty—1994*. Ottawa: The Canadian Council on Social Development.

Schragge, E. 1997. "Workfare: An Overview." In E. Schragge (ed.), *Workfare: Ideology for a New Under-Class*. Toronto: Garamond Press.

Segal, H. 1997. *Beyond Greed*. Toronto: Stoddart.

Statistics Canada. 1997a. *Canadian Economic Observer*. January. Catalogue No. 11-010-XPB.

———. 1997b. *Income Distributions by Size in Canada 1996*. Ottawa: Minister of Industry.

———. 1997c. *Low Income Persons 1980 To 1996 (Low Income Cut-offs, 1992 base)*. Ottawa: Minister of Industry.

———. 1997d. *Census Families in Private Households, 1991 and 1996*. (Catalogue 93-312). Ottawa: Statistics Canada.

———. 1997e. *Canadian Social Trends*. (Catalogue 11-008-XPE). Ottawa: Statistics Canada.

Swanson, J. 1998. "Child Poverty Focus Brings Policies that Push Down Wages." *NAPO News* 64.

Thompson, G. 1987. *Needs.* London: Rutledge and Kegan Paul.

United Nations Development Program (UNDP). 1991 to 1998. *Human Development Report.* New York-London: Oxford.

United Nations. 1989. *Convention on the Rights of the Child.* Ottawa: Minister of Supply & Services.

Ursel, J. 1992. *Private Lives, Public Policy, 100 Years of State Intervention in the Family.* Toronto: Women's Press.

Valpy, M. 1997. "A Down Payment, But Where Does it Lead." *The Globe and Mail* February 20, A21.

Vellekoop-Baldock, C. 1990. "Volunteerism and The Caring Role of Women." In C. Vellekoop-Baldoc (ed.), *Volunteers in Welfare.* Sydney: Allen and Unwin.

Walker, A., and C. Walker. 1997. *Britian Divided: The Growth of Social Exclusion in the 1980s and 1990s.* London: Child Poverty Action Group Ltd.

Zastrow, C. 1986. *Social Welfare Institutions: Social Problems, Services and Current Issues.* Third edition. Chicago, IL: The Dorsey Press.